The Psychology of Twinship

University of Nebraska Press: Lincoln and London

Ricardo C. Ainslie

The Psychology of
Twinship

The paper in this book meets
the guidelines for permanence
and durability of the
Committee on Production
Guidelines for Book
Longevity of the Council
on Library Resources.

Library of Congress
Cataloging in Publication Data

Ainslie, Ricardo C.
The psychology of twinship.

Bibliography: p.
Includes index.
1. Twins – Psychology.
I. Title. [DNLM:
1. Personality Development.
2. Twins – psychology.
WS 105.5.F2   A296p]
BF723.T9A34   1985
155.4'44   84-19591
ISBN 0-8032-1017-5
(alk. paper)

To Vern and Virginia

Contents

Preface

Twins have traditionally been viewed by researchers as providing an opportunity to explore the age-old question of genetic versus environmental influences on personality. The reason for this is readily apparent: by virtue of their genetic makeup, identical twins provide the only real controls for the genetic variable in human development. A common conclusion of this line of research has been that genetics contributes substantially to human psychological development. I do not take exception to this view. My working assumption is that genetics and environment both play an important role in this arena. My primary interest here, however, is on the environmental side of the equation, that is, in the characteristics of the developmental context of twinship and how these affect the psychological organization of twins.

It is fair to say that much twin research is not particularly concerned with twins as such but rather has found twins to be a suitable "device" for exploring more general questions. It is ironic that although twins have traditionally been a highly researched population, the literature that actually takes twins themselves as the object of interest is relatively scant. As Farber (1981) has pointed out, despite years of research, we still lack an adequate conceptualization for the psychological characteristics of twins and their origins. This book addresses this specific gap.

Although the principal aim of this work is to provide a better understanding of the environmental circumstances that tend to organize twin psychology, this exposition begins on ground that is most familiar to twin researchers, namely, the question of genetic inheritance of personality characteristics. In the first two chapters, genetic studies on twinship and personality development are reviewed and critiqued. In addition, the materials derived from identical-twin participants in this study are used to highlight the differences within identical twinships along a number of important personality dimensions. In this respect, twins are approached in the first portion of the book as they have been traditionally—as a medium through which the question of nature versus nurture can be properly magnified. There is a somewhat different emphasis here, however. Identical twins provide an excellent opportunity for examining environmental variables in personality development, since important differences between identical twins are best understood as having an environmental basis. The overall aim of these first two chapters, then, is to highlight the importance of environmental variables for personality development in twins.

The remainder of the book is directed toward clarifying and elaborating the developmental issues in twinship. The cornerstone of this effort is the third chapter, in which a variety of developmental theories are brought together to support the notion that twinship constitutes an altered developmental context. Specifically, I suggest that there are two junctures in early development during which twins are likely to experience an unusual amount of stress: one in early infancy roughly corresponds to Mahler's (1967) "normal symbiotic phase"; the other occurs toward the end of toddlerhood during Mahler's (1972) "rapprochement crisis." Although the basic conceptualizations proposed here draw heavily from psychoanalytic psychology, they also draw from other developmental perspectives. It is the convergence of perspectives that makes this conceptualization of twin development compelling.

The key factors that contribute to the psychology of twinship are to some extent independent of the genetic makeup (zygosity) of any particular twinship. In other words, the presence of two infants, faced with the same developmental needs and tasks, profoundly alters a child's usual environment. The manner in which people in the twins' environment are able to accommodate themselves to this altered context determines the degree to which twins are affected by this circumstance. Although zygosity may play a role in shaping parental perceptions, as some research suggests, it is not in and of itself the preeminent force in shaping twin development.

The middle chapters of this book elaborate this line of thinking. The theoretical conceptualization of twin development is tested against the presence of the psychological issues that one would postulate given this framework, such as identity confusion, separation and dependency, and role complementarity. The book also examines the fate of the twin relationship in adolescence and adulthood, with the aim of underscoring the fact that twins play a fundamentally important role in each other's psychological life. This discussion illustrates how the suggested developments during the twins' early years become integrated into a twin's personality. In a later chapter, the results of a survey of mothers of twins are presented in order to provide another perspective on early twin development. The final chapter integrates the findings of the earlier chapters.

A primary thesis of this work is that the developmental circumstances of twinship result in characteristic patterns of experiencing oneself and in characteristic psychological issues with which a twin must come to terms. I believe that it is accurate to speak of a specific psychology of twinship. However, the notion of a *specific* apart from a *unique* psychology of twinship must be distinguished. Twins are not fundamentally different from nontwins. Although the specific conditions of twin development lend themselves to specific characteristics of personality organization, nontwins raised under similar circumstances, for example, siblings who are quite close in age, may very closely resemble twins psychologically. In other words, my aim is not to further mythologize twins. On the contrary, the concepts that are brought forth to explain the developmental circumstances of twinship are drawn from established developmental theories.

The core of this work involves materials derived from what is sometimes termed life history research. Essentially I have attempted to apply a clinical interview methodology to a nonclinical population. I believe that the nature of the phenomena in question justifies such an approach. Newman, Freeman, and Holzinger (1937), for example, in discussing their failure to find significant results with a series of personality tests, conclude that the difficulty may be due to "subtle" characteristics of human relationships which "are revealed only by individual analysis" (p. 341). A clinical method makes such individual analysis possible in a way that more traditional methods of research do not. Why this is the case might become apparent as I describe the actual process in which the twins participated.

When possible, I interviewed both twins. Occasionally geographic considerations prevented the participation of both twins. During an initial conjoint interview with the twins, general questions regarding the twinship were asked. These included whether they were identical or fraternal, their birth order, and stories told about them as children. I further inquired about how they saw themselves as alike or different, how others saw them, the nature of their living circumstances, and how and if they felt being twins had affected their lives, and so on. All interviews were tape-recorded, so before subsequent interviews I would listen to the preceding interview to have a fresh impression of the material. In the individual interviews, I followed up and discussed various themes. However, the primary if often latent question posed to them was "What is it like to be a twin and how has it affected your life?" With the twin subjects, no formal questionnaire was used. The interviews were, for the most part, unstructured, although subjects were routinely asked about their developmental history as well as their early memories of themselves, their twins, and their parents. Otherwise, the interviews followed a clinical-evaluative format in which themes presented by the subjects were pursued as they appeared relevant and meaningful. Altogether, subjects were interviewed an average of three times. Some subjects—those who were particularly articulate and self-reflective—were interviewed up to five times. Each interview lasted approximately an hour and a half.

The analysis of the case material proceeded in the following manner: Tapes were first transcribed and then studied subject by subject, much as one would grapple with clinical material. Although the central interest was to understand the significance of twinship in the subjects' experience, the interpretations that I made from this material sometimes coincided with the subjects' views about themselves and sometimes did not. At these latter junctures, in writing conclusions, I have endeavored to present sufficient detail from the interviews so that readers might arrive at their own conclusions.

In presenting this study, I have attempted to achieve a balance between the "observance of the particulars," as Gordon Allport might have said, and general comments about the phenomenon in question. It is necessary to do justice to the former so that the reader obtains a living sense regarding individual material, yet it is also my intent to convey a picture that does not rest on case studies in isolation. Where possible, I attempt to go beyond the individual case to a more general statement about the psychology of twinship. In a sense, this process requires a constant movement between the sufficiency of detail in each case and more general observations across cases.

This study actually involves two different groups of subjects: twins and mothers of twins. Since each group was approached differently, I will describe the twin sample first.

A total of twenty-six twins participated in this study. (A descriptive table of the sample is presented in appendix A.) They ranged in age from fourteen to seventy-two (mean age = 27.8). The subjects represented fifteen different twinships. Nine were fraternal twins and seventeen were identical twins (by self-report).[1] With the exception of a pair of male identical twins, all of the twins who were asked to participate in the study agreed to do so. Regarding the pair who did not take part, one was adamant about not participating in the study, and his brother was reluctant to do so unilaterally. Two of the twins in this sample had been in psychotherapy, and following the interviews one of the subjects entered treatment. The sample is not intended to be random; it was obtained through informal referral, often through twins who knew other twins. The sample contains a higher incidence of identical twins than one would expect to find in a random sampling of the twin population; however, this is not altogether uncommon in twin research. In addition, the sample is predominantly Caucasian and middle-class.

The mothers who participated in this study were not the parents of

---

[1] This may be a source of criticism of the present work. There is some evidence, however, that self-report, including answers to such questions as "Were you and your twin ever confused by family members and other people?"—a question routinely posed to my subjects—coupled with degree of physical similarity, constitute fairly good predictors of actual zygosity in twins (Cederloff, Frieberg, Jonson, & Kaij, 1961). Even given significant error in the ascribed zygosity of my subjects, I believe that the primary thesis that I am presenting would remain largely intact since the central questions of this project are not genetic. This issue is further discussed in chapter 2.

my twin subjects. They were recruited through the Texas organization of Mothers of Multiples, and 130 of them responded to an extensive questionnaire (see appendix B). These questions ranged from purely demographic material, including the history of twins in the family of each of the parents, to detailed questions about their experience of parenting twins and strategies they used for handling various issues. For example, questions asked how the task of feeding the twins was accomplished during infancy, who the mothers' sources of support were, developmental milestones of each twin, and various other aspects of the experience of parenting twins. Since the great majority of the mothers had twins who were still under three years of age, their memories for most of the events were still relatively fresh.

The reader may question the generalizability of the findings. But this work does not generalize in the traditional sense of the term. Thus, I am not interested primarily in illustrating that certain phenomena appear in all twinships. Rather, I have selected from the interviews primary thematic areas and attempted to illustrate the various manifestations of each. Instead of correlating the presence of a global variable with twinship, I try to depict the subtle transformations and perspectives of that variable. For example, if the variable is associated with identity confusion, I have not set out to define this variable in a manner which I then apply to the subjects. Instead, I permit my subjects to define for us a portion of the "universe" of meanings which are associated with this variable. As some of the subjects render for us the *quality* of their identity confusion, we come to understand not only that *this* is a common feature of the psychology of twinship but, more important, *how* it is a factor in their experience of the world.

Finally, in order to obtain suitable material for this study, I felt that it was necessary to interact with my subjects—to inquire freely into areas that *they* might feel were important and to let them inform *me* about issues in twinship of which I might not be aware. In addition, I felt it was important to create a context within which I could, in a more clinical way, see firsthand the affects associated with certain topics or areas that were difficult to talk about. I wanted to witness their use of language and general styles of expression. And finally, I wanted to be able to see the twins together—to observe the interplay of their relationship. These interests dictated that an interview format would be the best choice of methodology for this project.

Acknowledgments

Work toward this book took place in two stages. The first portion of this project was my doctoral dissertation at the University of Michigan. Dr. George Rosenwald, the chairman of my committee, was and continues to be a source of inspiration as a model of scholarly thinking. Drs. Humberto Nagera and Antal Solyom, of the Children's Psychiatric Hospital at the University of Michigan Medical Center, were both very generous in their support and encouragement in my last years at Michigan. Further, I am grateful to Dr. Ivan Sherick, also of the Children's Psychiatric Hospital, for being the first to suggest that my work on twins might be worthy of a book.

The second phase of this project took place at the University of Texas at Austin, where a number of graduate students have been helpful in various aspects of the work. Special thanks are due to Dan O'Loughlin and Kelly Olmstead for their assistance with the analysis of the data from mothers of twins. I wish also to thank the University Research Institute at the University of Texas at Austin for their generous support for portions of this work.

A very special thanks to Dr. Robert Prall and Mary Jane Prall for their close reading of the manuscript as well as for the considerable support that they have extended to me.

Finally, I wish to thank my wife, Gemma, and my children, Roberto and Gabriella, for their affection and confidence, which were ever-present sources of sustenance.

1

Personality and Genetic Inheritance

Twinship constitutes a particular developmental context, although we know relatively little about it. As Farber (1981) has pointed out, despite years of research we still lack an adequate conceptualization of the psychological characteristics of twins and their origins. The best place to begin looking for the hallmarks of twin development is to examine existing twin research. This inquiry cannot be fully separated from the twin studies that have been interested primarily in genetics, however. Twinship has provided psychologists with an immensely rich source of information for understanding human behavior.

Twin birth is a unique circumstance. Some twins have identical genes because they come from a single egg. Such twins are said to be monozygotic, or identical. Other twin pairs—fraternal twins—come from two separate fertilized eggs and are said to be dizygotic. They are genetically no more alike than any nontwin sibling pair and have roughly 50 percent of their genes in common. This difference between monozygotic (MZ) and dizygotic (DZ) twins in the extent to which they share the same genetic makeup has made it possible, through a comparison of MZ and DZ twins, to explore the relative contribution of genetic and environmental factors to a variety of behaviors, dispositions, or traits. This is the essence of what is commonly termed the Twin Method. If the manifestation of a given characteristic is strongly under genetic control, then it is expected that MZ twins will be more alike on that dimension, since they are the same genetically. DZ twins, on the other hand, should be considerably less similar on the same dimension, since they are less similar genetically. By the same logic, differences between MZ pairs are understood to have an environmental source. The comparison of MZ and DZ twins has the added advantage of controlling a number of variables which would make comparisons between MZ twins and nontwin siblings diffi-cult—maternal age, sibling spacing, or the difficulties associated with measuring the same variables in children who are at different points in their development.

The Twin Method approach to the study of human behavior has been of great value in shedding light on the role of genetic contribu-tions to behavior, and the vast majority of research in which twins have participated has been in this tradition. However, it is fair to say that these studies, though informative, have told us comparatively little about twins themselves. After all, this research has not been research about twins but rather research about genetics. By examin-ing particular traits, and in comparing MZ and DZ twins, or twins and nontwin siblings, important dimensions of the twin situation itself emerge, although sometimes as by-products of research with a genetic focus. In addition, any study that explores the twin situation and hypothesizes about the nature of that developmental context has implications for genetic research as well because a key assumption of the Twin Method is that for all practical purposes twins share an equal environment. Hence, an exploration of the nature of that environ-ment is of interest to genetic researchers. Further, an examination of the role of environment in personality development highlights the extent to which variables are free to vary or the extent to which developmental contexts, if they do vary, can actually contribute to development. Because these research interests are interrelated, the best place to begin the exploration of the psychology of twinship is in the arena in which most twin research has taken place: the literature on genetic inheritance. This will afford us a considerably better posi-tion from which to evaluate what is known about twin development, what the issues are, and what facts must be accounted for by a developmental framework.

Genetic Studies

Twin studies have demonstrated quite convincingly that genes play a decisive role in the evolution of many human characteristics. The strongest evidence for genetic contributions to human development is found in studies that examine physical variables such as height, weight, and head size (i.e., anthropometric variables) and those that examine physiological processes. For example, studies looking at differences in height, comparing MZ twins and DZ twins, have consistently shown that height is under substantial genetic control.[1] Correlations between members of a twin pair for height tend to range from .90 to .96 for MZ twins, while correlations for DZ twins range from .44 to .64 (Burt, 1966; Mittler, 1971; Shields, 1962). Correlations for weight are similarly conclusive, ranging from .80 to .93 for MZ twins and from .51 to .63 for DZ twins (Burt, 1966; Mittler, 1971; Shields, 1962). Similar though somewhat weaker results have been reported on such variables as visually evoked potential (Dustman & Beck, 1965) and other perceptual tasks (e.g., G. Smith, 1949, Eysenck & Prell, 1951).

In psychology, a great deal of twin research has focused on the extent to which genetic factors contribute to intelligence. For example, Wilson (1977) compared MZ and DZ performance on the Wechsler Intelligence Scale for Children (WISC). He found that MZ's had a high degree of concordance for full-scale IQ (FIQ) and verbal IQ (VIQ). While DZ's had intermediate concordance, they were significantly below MZ's for concordance. In fact, DZ's were no more alike than nontwin siblings, which is what one would theoretically expect given that they have as many genes in common as any nontwin sibling pair. Other studies have found similar results (e.g., Erlenmeyer-Kimling & Jarvik, 1963; Loehlin & Nichols, 1976; Newman et al., 1937; Vernon, 1960).

Perhaps the strongest evidence for a genetic contribution to intelligence is offered by studies such as Shields (1962), in which he compared MZ twins who had been reared apart with MZ twins reared together. Because twins reared apart are exposed to different environments, one would expect lower intrapair correlations for variables that do not have a strong genetic basis, while variables that are strongly heritable would continue to show relatively high correlations. Shields

---

[1] Most heritability estimates are derived using intraclass correlations to compute Holzinger's H′ or heritability statistic. This is an estimate of the within-family variance attributable to heredity by comparing within-pair variance for MZ twins with within-pair variance for DZ twins. See Loehlin (1969) for a review of the statistical uses of Holzinger's H′.

found that intrapair IQ correlations for MZ twins reared together and those reared apart were similar. However, DZ twins reared together had considerably lower IQ correlations than either of the monozygotic groups.

Studies such as these cited here have tended to show that intelligence has a strong heritable component. Typically they have found intrapair correlations to be in the .60's and .70's, although sometimes lower as well. However, the complexity involved in interpreting these results is reflected in studies focusing on achievement that have shown considerably weaker results. To cite one such example, in comparing MZ twins reared together, MZ twins reared apart, and DZ twins reared together on intellectual potential, Burt (1966) found high intraclass correlations for MZ twins, whether reared together or apart (.92 and .87, respectively), with DZ twins having considerably lower correlations (.53). However, similar results were not found when he compared the twins in terms of their level of attainment (reading, spelling, and arithmetic). Here, Burt found that MZ twins reared together continued to have the highest intraclass correlations; however, DZ twins had consistently higher correlations than MZ twins reared apart. Thus, these results would suggest that level of attainment is strongly influenced by environmental factors in addition to whatever genetic factors are at play. Newman et al. (1937) reported similar results.

Studies that have used Thurstone's Primary Abilities (PMA) test have shown conflicting results and considerable differences in heritability across studies (e.g., Thurstone, Thurstone, & Strandkov, 1955; Vandenberg, 1962, 1965). Vandenberg's (1966) comparison of these studies shows almost no consistency in the estimation of the heritability of each of Thurstone's six PMA factors (verbal, reasoning, word fluency, space, number, memory). The estimate of heritability for the factor "number" varied by as much as .54 (.07 for Blewett's 1954 study versus .61 in Vandenberg's 1962 study). In his review of these studies, Mittler (1971) aptly remarks that the discrepancies in these studies may have a number of sources. For example, none of them analyzed the sample by sex, even though the samples varied considerably on this dimension and a number of cognitive processes, especially those related to language, have been found to show sex differences. Studies have also varied considerably in terms of design and ages of the populations studied. These differences may account for some of the variability, but it is unlikely that all of the variation can be accounted for by methodological artifact. In short, heritability estimates for intellectual and cognitive processes have been lower than those for anthropometric studies, and they have been much more inconsistent when specific factors are examined.

Burt's findings reflect the overall trends in the literature: namely, there appear to be clear-cut genetic contributions to intelligence scores, but there are also clear-cut environmental contributions to the extent to which variations in genetic endowment can actually be put into practice, as measured by the attainment scores. Clearly, there is an interaction between environmental and genetic factors.

Viewed from another perspective, we find increasing environmental contribution as we move away from anthropometric variables toward variables that are more psychological. For example, in his study using the Illinois Test of Psycholinguistic Abilities (ITPA), Mittler (1971) found that between 44 percent and 69 percent of the variance of the total ITPA score was genetic in origin. This means that approximately one-third to one-half of the variance in these scores is due primarily to environmental factors.

The role of genetic contribution to human development follows a continuum. Here, anthropometric variables demonstrate the strongest contribution, while intellectual and ability measures represent an intermediate point. However, with few exceptions, the case for a substantial genetic contribution has been the weakest for variables associated with personality and temperament.

In 1937 Newman et al. raised the question whether personality factors have a major genetic component at all. The basis for the question rests on the fact that demonstration of genetic factors in this arena has been most elusive. Yet positive indications of genetic contribution have been found in several studies, especially those looking at temperament. Here lies the strongest case for genetic factors in personality.

Researchers have looked at different dimensions of temperament in exploring the role of genetic factors. These studies have not been particularly consistent in approach: some have used a variety of objective personality inventories, while others have used parental questionnaires. Further, the subjects in these studies have ranged in age from infancy to adulthood. Thus, for a variety of reasons, clear-cut comparisons are difficult to make. Nevertheless, results have not been altogether inconsistent for some aspects of temperament.

One of the variables that has been studied with some consistency is level of activity. For example, Buss, Plomin, and Willerman (1973) constructed a questionnaire assessing, among other variables, *activity* defined as "the sheer amount of response output" (p. 514). They included among the items such descriptions as "child is off and running as soon as he wakes up in the morning," and "child is always on the go" (p. 517). Five such questions were asked in relation to each temperament. Mothers completed the questionnaire for twins ranging in age from four months to sixteen years (mean age = fifty-five months). The authors found that intraclass correlations for MZ twins were significantly higher when compared with DZ twins (.87 versus .17 for boys; .71 versus .14 for girls). Buss et al. concluded that activity had a strong genetic component.

Rutter, Korn, and Birch (1963) looked at a small sample of twins (N = 8) longitudinally, assessing what they termed *primary reaction patterns*, including activity. The data for their study were derived from detailed narrative accounts by parents of their child's daily behavior over time. All of the children were at least two years old at the time of the analysis. Rutter et al. employed a rigorous set of criteria for a characteristic to be considered largely genetic: (1) as with most studies, MZ twins had to be more alike than DZ twins; (2) DZ twins had to be more alike than nontwin siblings; and (3) no large differences should be found within MZ pairs. Of the seven variables considered, activity was one of three with the strongest evidence for genetic contribution, fulfilling two of the three criteria (no variables fulfilled all three criteria). On the activity dimension, MZ twins were found to be more alike than DZ twins, and DZ twins were more alike than nontwin siblings.

In a fairly detailed study of activity motivation, Scarr (1966) found considerable evidence of genetic contribution. Scarr's subjects were all Caucasian girls between the ages of six and ten. Scarr's interest was to focus on activity level, specifically on individual differences in how much activity per se was initiated, how rapidly or slowly, how often, and with how much vigor or apathy, among other things. Measures of activity motivation were obtained from The Toys game (adapted from

Smock & Holt, 1962) and The Slides game (Berlyne, 1960). In addition, an interview with the children and a number of rating scales, including Gough's (1960) Adjective Check List (ACL), were used. Scarr found that for all five measures of preferred reaction time derived from the two games, which she assumed were an index of activity motivation, MZ twins had higher intraclass correlations than DZ twins (heritability estimates for these variables ranged from .24 to .40). In addition, intraclass coefficients for total different activities (derived from the interviews) were considerably higher for MZ than for DZ twins. Here the heritability estimate was 40 percent, suggesting that variation in *number* of activities in which a child engaged was determined in part by genetic factors. Scarr's results imply a consistent, if moderate, genetic contribution to these behaviors.

As a final example of studies examining the genetic contribution to activity level, Torgersen and Kringlen (1978) conducted a study in which twin pairs were assessed on a number of temperament variables, including activity level, when twins were two months and nine months of age. Torgersen and Kringlen analyzed mother interviews and found that by nine months MZ twins were significantly more similar ($p < .001$) than DZ twins on the activity dimension.

The results from these studies are representative of other research (e.g., Vandenberg, 1962; Plomin, 1976; Plomin & Rowe, 1977) which has consistently found evidence for a moderate to strong genetic contribution to the temperament variable of activity level. Not all of the results have been unambiguous, however. For example, Rutter et al. did find some MZ twinships in which there were large differences in activity (lack of such large differences was one of their criteria for evidence of a strong genetic contribution). In addition, their results indicated, paradoxically, that the variables that seemed to have the strongest genetic profile (including activity) were also the variables that were least stable over time. One would expect variables strongly under genetic control to be more stable, not less. Nevertheless, the Rutter et al. study can be interpreted as lending at least some support to the view that level of activity is strongly influenced by genetic factors.

Scarr's study also raises a number of questions regarding the meaning of the activity construct. For example, although she found that the number of activities in which a child engaged was determined in part by genetic factors, she also found that the *kinds* of games, such as active or sedentary ones, "were not affected at all by genetics" (p. 670). It is not clear, however, why activity level, if indeed it does have a strong genetic component, would not also be manifested in the kinds of games a child might play. The latter raises a question which is often taken for granted: namely, it is not clear, especially from studies using a variety of inventories, what relationship differential scores, on any given variable, have to actual behaviors and attitudes.

Sociability is the variable for which findings of a strong genetic component have been most consistent. This variable has been studied in a number of different ways. As part of the study reported earlier, Scarr (1969) also rated twin girls on the Fels Child Behavior Scales (Richards & Simons, 1941) and Gough's (1960) Adjective Check List. All of the sociability measures showed MZ twins to be significantly more alike than DZ twins ($p<.01$ to $p<.001$), with heritability estimates ranging from .55 to .83. Several of the other studies of temperament I have reviewed here also included the variable of sociability. All found sociability to have a strong genetic component. For example, Buss et al. (1973) as well as Plomin and Rowe (1977) report intraclass correlations for MZ twins to be significantly higher than those for DZ twins at the $p<.01$ level. Eysenck (1956), Vandenberg (1962, 1966), and Gottesman (1963, 1966) have all reported similar findings, using a variety of instruments.

Studies that looked at specific dimensions within sociability (Scarr, 1969, would be an exception) reported more varied results. For example Wilson, Brown, and Matheny (1971) conducted a longitudinal study, collecting maternal reports on their twins. Mothers were interviewed when their twins were three, six, nine, twelve, eighteen, twenty-four, thirty, and thirty-six months old, after which they were interviewed yearly until the twins were five years old. While overall differences were in the expected direction (i.e., genetic), significant differences in concordance were not found for such variables as *smiling*, *seeking affection*, or *accepting people*. The one exception was a significant difference between MZ and DZ twins on seeking affection between twenty-four and thirty months (this means that there was one significant difference out of fifteen reported scores on these three variables, and thus quite possibly a chance finding). In a different study, Brown, Stafford, and Vandenberg (1967) also did not find a significant difference between MZ and DZ twins on the variable *laughs, smiles more readily*. These results are somewhat surprising for behaviors that one would expect to have a strong relationship to sociability.

Plomin and Rowe's (1979) study of social behavior in infancy, described in greater detail shortly, found supportive evidence for Buss and Plomin's (1975) suggestion that sociability might best be thought of as having two components: quantity (as in gregariousness) and quality (denoting warmth or affection with familiar figures). Plomin and Rowe studied infants' behaviors with their mothers and their response to the presence of a stranger during home observations. Their results indicated that children's reactions to the stranger (i.e., the quantity dimension of sociability) appeared to have a strong genetic component, while their interactions with their mother (the quality dimension of sociability) did not. It may be that a mother filling out a questionnaire about her children's sociability might have been thinking about their relationship to her (i.e., the qualitative dimensions) rather than their behavior toward other people, hence the relatively lower concordance for MZ twins on specific items that would appear to be related to sociability.

Thus, with a few exceptions, studies that have examined sociability have found it to have a strong heritable component. These findings have been consistent across a range of studies using different instruments and using different age groups. Among the other variables which have been shown to have at least a moderate genetic component are *adaptability* (Rutter et al., 1963; Matheny & Dolan, 1975; Wilson & Matheny, 1983; Buss et al., 1973); *distractability* (Rutter et al., 1963; Matheny, Wilson, Dolan, & Krantz, 1981; Matheny & Dolan, 1975); *impulsivity* (Plomin, 1976; Buss et al., 1973); *intensity* (Wilson & Matheny, 1983; Torgensen & Kringlen, 1978); and *emotionality* (Plomin, 1976; Buss et al., 1973).

Although not exhaustive, this review reflects a broad literature that underscores the significance of genetic factors in personality and temperament variables. However, even these studies reflect the difficulties in assessing genetic influence in this domain. For example, in the Buss et al. (1973) study, impulsivity was found to have stronger correlations among female DZ twins than MZ twins, a finding that would run counter to the genetic hypothesis and is difficult to interpret. Further, these results may be somewhat at variance with those of Torgersen and Kringlen (1978), who found stronger correlations between MZ twins for *intensity of response* and *threshold of responsiveness*, two variables persumably related to impulsivity. In addition, Buss et al. found a general trend for heritabilities to be higher for boys than for girls on three of the four temperaments studied. Sex differences in heritabilities have been reported by other researchers as well (e.g., Gottesman, 1963; Nichols, 1966; Loehlin & Nichols, 1976), a finding that has not been adequately explained by twin researchers except to suggest that, in principle, there is no reason to assume an equal heritability potential for both genders.

Further, some results have been contradictory. For example, Plomin and Rowe (1977) found that reaction to food was not a heritable response. In contradistinction to this, Wilson et al. (1971) found strong food preferences and poor appetite to be heritable.

Generally, the support for a *strong* genetic component is tenuous in these studies. Concordance rates, for example, do not tend to go above 60 percent for many of the variables that have consistently been found to have a genetic contribution, thereby leaving considerable room for the role of environmental factors. Often there is little agreement as to which specific scales within a given instrument are heritable and which are not; within studies there is little agreement between the sexes as to which variables are significantly heritable; and for some factors the overall differences between MZ and DZ twins are *too* large to fit the genetic hypothesis (Loehlin, 1969). Because of this, most researchers have concluded that even variables with the strongest genetic evidence also manifest the importance of environmental contributions. Clearly, environmental and genetic factors act in concert with one another to shape dimensions of personality.

The contribution of environmental factors to psychological development is supported by research that reports a decrease in the genetic contribution to particular traits over time. Such a decrease in concordance for MZ twins underlines the increased importance of environment, since increased environmental exposure creates greater variability in the expression of that trait. Buss et al. (1973) report such decreases. As noted earlier, they found significantly higher correlations for MZ twins over DZ twins on the four temperaments studied (with the exception of impulsivity in DZ girls). But when they divided their sample into two groups to see if there were differences by age, they found that for emotionality all correlations increased with age, but for the rest of the temperaments, correlations decreased with age for both MZ and DZ twins, suggesting greater environmental influence.

From a slightly different vantage, Dworkin, Burke, Maher, and Gottesman (1977) found results that underscore the same point. They compared the significance of correlations between MZ and DZ twins longitudinally using the California Personality Inventory (CPI) and the Minnesota Multiphasic Personality Inventory (MMPI) during adolescence and twelve years later when their subjects were adults. They found that only a few of the scales on either test showed stability over time (the dependency and anxiety subscales of the MMPI and the dominance subscale of the CPI). In fact, most of the subscales that had been found to be significant at adolescence lost that significance in adulthood, thereby reflecting decreasing genetic expression. Buss et al. reported similar findings.

In another longitudinal study, Wilson et al. (1971) found similar results. Although there was considerable continuity in three nuclear clusters of variables over time (sociability, temperament, and vocalization), the interrelationships had weakened by the time the twins were forty-eight months of age, again suggesting an increased environmental contribution. Interestingly, Wilson et al. also found that concordance rates for temper frequency, temper intensity, irritability, and crying for *both* MZ and DZ twins actually increased with age. This suggests that environmental effects were at work to make twin pairs in both kinds of twinships more like one another.

A number of studies showed a lack of significant results in the realm of personality variables. Rutter et al. (1963), for example, did find evidence of substantial genetic influence in three of the seven temperament categories that they studied; however, they were actually more impressed by the role of nongenetic factors. A study by Lytton (1980) is among the most comprehensive to be found in the twin literature. The depth with which Lytton approached the subject is unusual. In this project twins were assessed in a variety of ways, including extensive home observations, laboratory observations, testing, and extensive interviews with the mothers. Although Lytton reports a number of interesting findings (discussed below), on the whole he found that, even after extensive and complex analyses, "the genetic harvest [was] meager." The variance for most variables studied was accounted for by error, individual experiences, and environmental differences between families.

Similarly, a number of studies involving the MMPI and the Junior Personality Questionnaire (JPQ) have also failed to show strong genetic findings. No variables on these two tests were significant across all three studies summarized by Vandenberg (1967). Dworkin et al. (1977) found only two of the MMPI subscales and only one CPI score to be significant at retesting. Gottesman (1963) found that although comparisons on all of the twenty-four traits that he studied (ten factors from the MMPI and fourteen factors from the High School Personality Questionnaire) were in the direction predicted, only six appeared to be significantly influenced by genetic factors (that is, correlations between the scores of MZ twins were significantly higher than those of DZ twins). Gottesman estimated that altogether eleven of the twenty-four traits showed at least *some* appreciable genetic component. What this means, of course, is that environmental effects account for most of the remaining variance, which is substantial. Gottesman concluded that environment appeared to be the preponderant influence in a majority of traits which he measured. Lytton (1980) drew a similar conclusion: "The hard fact is that genetic factors, particularly in human social characteristics, are extremely elusive and hard to demonstrate in replicable form in empirical genetic investigations" (p. 268).

That environmental factors play a major role in most personality traits seems to be accepted by the majority of researchers. As Gottesman (1963) has suggested, heredity can best be thought of as fixing a reaction range. Within this range, there is room for variation in the expression of genetically determined factors as a function of environmental circumstances. In terms of personality variables, this room appears to be substantial.

The closer the variables under consideration correspond to physical measures, such as body size, the stronger and clearer the genetic contribution. Variables related to intellectual processes, such as intelligence and ability or achievement, form an intermediate group in terms of the strength of genetic contribution. Personality and temperament studies have also found evidence of genetic contribution, although here the genetic factor appears to be much less, a fact which is reflected in lower heritability estimates and less consistent results. Personality variables, standing at the opposite end of the continuum from anthropometric variables, are shaped to a greater extent by environmental factors than by genetics.

The findings from this literature are important to us because they emphasize that, for personality development, environmental factors must be taken into account. Thus alerted, we are now in a position to ask what it has to tell us about the specific circumstances of twinship and the effects of these circumstances on twin development.

Psychological Factors in Twinship

How similar are twins? If MZ twins are dissimilar, then, as we have seen, it implicates environment in the process of human development. The stronger the case for such environmental factors, the stronger the need to *understand* what those factors may be in the context of twinship.

Many studies have, in fact, found twins to be discordant or complementary for some personality variables. Allen, Greenspan, & Pollin (1976) followed a relatively small sample of twins (N = 10) longitudinally with in-depth interviews, behavioral ratings, and other measures. Among their findings was the observation that although MZ twins are genetically the same, and in many ways remarkably similar, parents were aware of differences between them. These mothers consistently perceived their twins as being sharply differentiated along a number of dimensions, including temperament. Among the observations noted were (1) differences in the relative ease of adaptation for one twin to new situations, including a difference in initial fearfulness; (2) a tendency for one twin to be relatively more methodical and thoughtful, the other more excitable and emotional; (3) a difference in objective orientation, one twin appearing to be more interested in people (sociable) and the other more oriented toward inanimate objects; (4) a difference in approach to the environment, one twin tending to explore patiently and thoroughly, the other more actively searching for some new stimulation; and (5) a tendency for one twin to be more passive, the other more confident and assertive. Allen and his co-workers found that in six of the ten families studied, important environmental events had occurred during the first year which significantly differentiated the twins. For example, these authors found that the twin who had suffered a major neonatal illness tended to be less curious, less active, less sociable, more dependent, and less dominant. Numerous other authors have reported a similar capacity on the part of parents to differentiate their twins (e.g., Mittler, 1971; Lytton, 1980; Wilson & Matheny, 1983). Lytton, for example, found that thirty-five of forty-six mothers of twins identified one of their twins as clearly more dominant than the other.

Wilson et al. (1971) report at length about the discrepancies that they encountered in some MZ twin pairs. They note that in discordant pairs one twin was much more prone to manifold expressions of temper and distress. Longer attention span for the less temperamental twin was also noted. Some twins were talkative, responsive to others, and actively sought attention, while their co-twins tended to be detached, less affectionate, and more irritable. According to Wilson et al., this was the prototype for the discordant twins. Further, these authors noted that after twelve months the complementary character of many of the twin relationships had become relatively stable as interpersonal patterns. "Once the members of a pair have established their positions on a particular variable—e.g., twin A crying more than twin B—they are likely to maintain that relationship and be classified the same way at the next age" (p. 1387). In fact, for a study of genetic variables, these authors devote considerable attention to the areas of discordance in their subjects, concluding that "the sizeable number of discordant monozygotic pairs" makes it clear that experiential factors must contribute substantially to temperament (p. 1393). A few other reports in the literature support the view that MZ twins may be different from one another in important ways. For example, Gesell and Thompson (1941) in looking at individual differ- ences in a pair of MZ twins from infancy to adolescence found one of them to be consistently more sociable than her twin, who appeared to be more intellectually inclined. Freedman and Keller (1963) have reported similar observations.

The results of Gottesman (1963) can be interpreted as supporting the view that MZ twins may be different on a number of important dimensions. When comparing overall MMPI profiles, Gottesman found ten of thirty-four twins to have profiles that were quite dissimilar to one another, while twelve of thirty-four DZ twin profiles were classified as similar. These findings have important implications for our understanding of the role of environmental factors. First, they indicate that environmental factors serve to differentiate MZ twins along broad dimensions of personality. However, they also emphasize that it is an error to interpret MZ similarity exclusively as being genetic in origin. If environmental factors serve to make DZ twins more similar along some personality dimensions, at least in this "holistic" approach to the MMPI, then it is reasonable to assume that they can affect MZ twins in the same manner. Lytton (1980) noted that at times twin behavior appeared to be quite "infectious," which led him to wonder whether this might account for some of the similarity found in twins.

The findings of some studies suggest that the twin situation might actually force a degree of differentiation between twins along certain dimensions. Vandenberg and Johnson (1968) gathered results from previous intelligence studies involving twins reared apart and re-analyzed them by looking at the length of time that twins had been separated from one another. They divided twins on the basis of whether they had been separated within the first six months or had spent a year or more together in the same environment. Interestingly, they found that those twins who had lived together the longest before being separated were actually more different in terms of IQ than twins who had been separated from an early age (an average difference of 9.59 IQ points as opposed to 5.5 IQ points). These findings, then, appear to support *both* a genetic and an environmental position. MZ twins who are reared apart remain similar to one another. However, MZ twins reared together were made more different by their environment.

In the study of social behaviors in infancy by Plomin and Rowe (1979) described earlier, the authors found that environmental factors, especially those within the family, played a key role in MZ and DZ twinships. Positive vocalization toward mother, smiling at mother, and cuddliness with stranger all had significant correlations for *both* MZ and DZ twins, suggesting within-family influences. Furthermore, they found no significant differences in the correlations between the two groups of twins on these variables. A study by Lytton, Martin, and Evans (1977), involving an attachment measure with children of approximately the same age as those in the Plomin and Rowe study, also showed a predominance of within-family environmental variance.

The studies discussed thus far suggest that there are important environmental factors at work in twin development. Other studies, however, indicate that the twin situation has specific developmental consequences for twins. For example, numerous IQ studies involving twins have consistently found that, on average, twins show lower IQ scores than singletons (children born singly) especially in the verbal area (e.g., Record, McKeown, & Edwards, 1970; Koch, 1966; Breland, 1973). In addition, studies that have specifically looked at twin language development have consistently shown deficits for twins (e.g., Conway, Lytton, & Pysh, 1980; Day, 1932; Mittler, 1970, 1971; Record et al., 1970). Twin language is reported to be slower to develop and to be more immature than that of singletons. Day (1932) found twins to have a poorer vocabulary and to use less complex sentences. These effects were reported to increase with age and were believed to be more extensive than simple IQ scores would suggest. Record et al. compared intact twin pairs with twins who had been raised as single children because their co-twin was stillborn. Stresses associated with a twin birth and variations in birth weight made both groups of twins comparable. On this basis, Record et al. concluded that postnatal factors were the most likely source of lowered twin IQ scores. An exception to these findings is Wilson (1975), who reported that by age six IQ differences between twins and singletons, as measured on the Wechsler Preschool and Primary Scale of Intelligence, had disappeared.

What in the twin situation would account for the reported deficits? In a study that included extensive home observations, Lytton (1980) found marked differences in the amount of speech that mothers and fathers of twins directed toward them when compared with singletons. There was a trend for parents to initiate less speech toward their twins, both in rate of speech per minute and in percentage of total verbalizations. Twins also initiated significantly less speech toward their parents than did singletons and, as in the studies just cited, their speech was judged to be less mature. These findings strongly suggest that the developmental context of twinship contributes to the language difficulties found in twins.

In another report from the same data, Conway et al. (1980) further suggested that the difficulties in speech found in twins were due at least partly to pressures on the mother but also to the fact that twins are a close-knit pair and therefore less verbally interactive with her. This would suggest that the closeness of the twinship may interfere with twin linguistic development. Twins having a private language may be a specific illustration of this observation, insofar as the twin relationship temporarily preempts or limits verbal interaction with others. It would appear that the presence of two children at the same developmental stage creates certain changes in the "average expectable environment" which contribute to the language difficulties often noted in twins.

Other supportive evidence for the hypothesis that the twin situation contributes to deficits in language development is not hard to find. Luria and Yudovitch (1959) found that the noted deficits in language development in twins diminished considerably when one compared twins who had been separated. Although these results were confounded by an educational intervention, other findings also support the conclusions. In the study by Record et al. (1970), twins whose co-twin had been stillborn, and hence who had been raised as singletons, were found to have IQ scores higher (nearly the same as those of singletons) than those of the intact twin pairs. In his work involving scores on the National Merit Scholarship Examination, Breland (1973) found that the closer the nontwin siblings are spaced, the more likely they are to be at an intellectual disadvantage, especially in the verbal sphere. This finding held true when twins were looked at specifically, since they ranked low when compared with other possible family configurations. Zazzo (1960) found that the 7-point IQ difference between twins and singletons reported in his sample dropped to 2.25 points when siblings who were close in age were used as the comparison group.

Other studies have also reported important differences between twins and singletons. For example, in nursery school observations, Kim, Dales, Connor, Walters, and Witherspoon (1969) found twins to be less affectionate, less aggressive, and more solitary than singletons at age three and a half. When they retested these same children at age five and a half, none of these differences remained significant. As Sroufe and Waters (1977) have noted, behaviors that may constitute a more or less adequate measure of a trait at one age may not correspond to the behaviors that would best assess that same trait later, since behaviors related to the expression of those particular characteristics change over time. This may account for the absence of differences at age five and a half in the Kim et al. study. However, it is also possible that, like Wilson's (1975) findings for IQ, developmental lags that appear early in twin development are made up by the time a child is nearly six years old. Nevertheless, at the very least, the Kim et al. findings suggest that some contextual factors are at play early in twins' development which may affect them on important social dimensions in the early years.

The few studies that looked at attachment in twins found twins to be different from singly born children in important respects. In Lytton's (1980) study reviewed above, findings related to language development and the twin situation were emphasized. In addition, however, Lytton also looked closely at the attachment patterns of twins (average age = 2.8 years) and found important differences. For twins with both mother-attachment and father-attachment data available (from home observation ratings of approaching, touching, seeking attention, and seeking help), there was an overall trend toward greater mother attachment. But a striking proportion of the twins also had an attachment rate toward father that was greater than that toward mother. Of seventy-six twins, forty-nine were classified as mother-attached, while twenty-seven were classified as father-attached. Lytton further noted that there was "a much greater likelihood for twins to take father as their preferred attachment object than for singletons to do so" (p. 117). Lytton hypothesized that this might be due to the greater competition for mother's time and attention in the context of twinship. In almost half of the twinships in which there was a father-attached twin, each twin appeared to have gravitated toward his or her favorite parent: one twin was father-attached, the other mother-attached. In at least one instance, the difference between the father-attached and the mother-attached twin was quite marked, resulting in the observation that the mother-attached twin "never emitted any attachment behaviors to the father at all" (p. 117).

Plomin and Rowe's (1979) observations would appear to lend support to Lytton's results. They found that the twins' attachment behaviors toward their mother appeared to be primarily environmental (within-family) rather than genetic, reflected in lower intrapair cor-relations for MZ twins. Of course what this means is that for some MZ twins there were substantial differences in the quality of each twin's attachment to mother.

This chapter has approached the psychology of twinship from two perspectives: First, I examined the literature on genetic inheritance for a clarification of the relative contribution of environmental and ge-netic factors in personality. Second, I examined these and other stud-ies involving twins for their contribution to our understanding of twinship itself as a developmental context. The results can be summa-rized as follows: In the realm of personality development, environ-ment appears to play an important role in shaping and directing whatever genetic predispositions may be present for a given trait, even those that have been found to have a strong genetic component. In addition, the literature reviewed strongly suggests that the twin situation itself exerts a number of specific influences on twin develop-ment. This is reflected in language development and IQ, for example, but it is also consistently reported by researchers who have made close observations of twins on various socially embedded psychological dimensions.

The interest here is less in the question of whether nature or nurture is preeminent. However, findings which indicate that environmental factors are important in personality development specifically serve to bring into relief the question of the developmental context of twin-ship itself.

2

Identical Twins and Personality Characteristics

This chapter looks in greater detail at some of the differences in identical twinships along personality dimensions. These differences will highlight the environmental contribution to personality development. I also intend, though somewhat more implicitly, to begin to give the reader a flavor for the psychology of twins that is more organically tied to the twin experience. We often lose a more immediate sense for data when it is presented by way of scales and structured questionnaires. Comparability and methodological consistency is gained but frequently at the expense of direct appreciation for the phenomena in question. For example, it is difficult to understand the implication of differences between MZ twins on the MMPI or CPI, except in terms that are somewhat abstract. Remember that these differences are related to real dimensions which are part of the ordinary day-to-day living for twins. Without such a direct relationship, objective studies are of limited value. Because direct interview material will be used in this chapter to illustrate the differences between identical twins, the aims of highlighting environmental factors in identical twinships and providing a more immediate picture of twin psychology are intimately interrelated.

Zygosity was determined in this sample by using the twins' self-description—whether they were ever confused by others, ever confused by family—and by observing the degree of physical similarity—except in those cases where both twins didn't participate in the study. Similar criteria have been used by a number of researchers with good results when compared with actual zygosity as determined by extensive blood-typing (see Cederloff, Frieberg, Jonson, & Kaij, 1961; Cohen, Dibble, Grawe, & Pollin, 1975; Nichols & Bilbro,

1966, for a discussion of assessment of zygosity via methods that do not involve blood-typing). These methods have been found to be reliable and have been used in many of the twin studies reported in the literature, but they are not foolproof. According to these studies, a misdiagnosis of actual zygosity might be expected in 7 to 15 percent of the cases. Thus, it is possible that a small proportion of the same-sex twin pairs in this study may be misdiagnosed. However, the main thesis of this book does not depend on error-free zygosity determination.

To illustrate the importance of environmental factors in twin development, data from MZ twins that emphasize their differences will be presented. Specifically, material derived from the twin interviews will be contrasted with two dimensions discussed in the genetic literature: *sociability*, which has consistently been found to have a relatively strong genetic component; and *dominance*, for which evidence of a strong genetic component is weaker. These two dimensions have been selected because a variety of studies have reported findings relevant to them (especially sociability) and because the content was similar between the interview data and the genetic literature on these points. Other possible issues that could have been discussed, such as findings related to the psychopathic deviate scale of the MMPI for which Gottesman (1963) found a relatively high heritability estimate ($H' = .50$), are excessively narrow in scope. Sociability and dominance, for example, are more generic constructs and are easily discussed as universal traits around which individuals vary.

Sociability is one characteristic on which a number of the twins who participated in this study seemed to differ. Buss and Plomin (1975) suggested that sociability might best be thought of as having two components: one relating to quantity, the other to quality. Employing observations of twins interacting with their mother and a stranger, Plomin and Rowe (1979) found evidence supportive of this conceptualization of sociability. The present interview data do not lend themselves easily to a definitive clarification of this distinction. However, many twins appeared to be quite different from each other in terms of sociability, broadly defined as a greater openness toward others, tending to be liked by others, or an inclination toward having long-term relationships with others. The increased openness toward others and possibly differences in likability would coincide with the quantity dimension of sociability, while the depth of relationships might be interpreted as coinciding with the quality dimension.

There was no clear-cut distinction along these two dimensions for the MZ twins who participated in this study. Some twins appeared to be concordant for the quantity dimension (e.g., both were quite popular in high school) while others appeared discordant (e.g., one had many friends, the other did not). However, this may be due to methodological artifacts such as the smallness of the sample that was interviewed. Nonetheless, the data presented in this chapter do provide some interesting descriptions of variables or characteristics related to the construct of sociability. Before turning to the interview data, let us examine some of the other reports in the literature which bear on sociability.

A number of researchers have found evidence for a relatively strong genetic contribution to sociability, broadly defined. Gottesman (1963) found the social introversion scale of the MMPI to be the most heritable of the instrument's ten clinical scales and six experimental scales, with the variance accounted for by hereditary factors of $H = .71$. Gottesman's analysis of the High School Personality Questionnaire (HSPQ) permits a greater degree of differentiation of the sociability construct, since several of the HSPQ scales might be seen as representing different vantage points on social relations or social inclination on the part of the subject; for example, stiff and aloof versus warm and sociable, or shy and sensitive versus adventurous and thickskinned, or group dependency versus self-sufficiency. Gottesman found that although most of the MZ-DZ differences on the HSPQ were in the predicted (i.e., genetic) direction, only the measure of group dependence versus self-sufficiency showed a significant difference between them ($H' = .56$).

The HSPQ and the MMPI scales are not directly comparable since they ask different questions and may therefore be tapping different aspects of sociability. However the scale for stiff and aloof versus warm and sociable and the scale for shy and sensitive versus adventurous and thickskinned from the HSPQ, which appear to be closest to the social introversion scale of the MMPI, had relatively low heritability estimates (.10 and .38, respectively). In another study, Gottesman (1966) found a heritability estimate of .49 for the sociability scale of the California Personality Inventory (CPI) and a slightly lower one for the social presence scale ($H' = .35$).

As reported in chapter 1, Scarr (1969) used a variety of measures, including interviews, standard tests, and experimental games, in her study of social introversion-extroversion. Mothers completed the Adjective Check List (Gough, 1960) on both twins (all girls between the ages of six and ten). Experimenters also rated the twins independently on several of the Fels Child Behavior Scales (Richards & Simons, 1941). Scarr's study specifically examined such dimensions as sociability, social anxiety, friendliness to strangers, and social spontaneity. She found a number of these dimensions to be heritable. Among the strongly heritable scales were need affiliation on the Adjective Check List, $H' = .61$, friendliness (.78) and social apprehension (.83) on the Fels scale, and the observer rating of likableness ($H' = .61$). Other studies have reported similar results using different instruments (e.g., Eysenck, 1956; Vandenberg, 1962, 1966).

But how do these variations or similarities actually appear in the lives of twins? The interviews suggest that consideration of characteristics related to sociability is a very complicated matter. Take, for example, one subject's description of how he and his twin brother function in social situations:

Tom: "In social activities that we do together, such as work, church, or choir, we like people, getting to know people. I'd say we act fairly similarly in those situations. I can say one thing, I think I'm more willing to talk and do things when we're together than when I'm alone, because Tim and I, thinking alike and doing things alike, at least I've got Tim that's there to back me up, to do the same thing, join in the conversation-type thing. So when I'm alone, I'm a little more reserved about what I'll say or do."

This description goes right to the heart of the difficulties inherent in interpreting subjects' responses to questionnaires or scales. It is unclear from Tom's response whether these twins are concordant or discordant for the characteristics described. The interpretation of this would seem to hinge on our understanding of the relationship itself. For example, if Tim, too, feels less reserved or shy in social situations that *include* Tom, but more so when he is without Tom, then the twins would appear to be concordant (both might be considered shy). However, if Tim feels more comfortable in social circumstances in the first place, then they would be discordant, even though their behavior may be manifestly similar in a social situation involving both twins. Were Tom filling out a questionnaire about his behavior in social situations, it is likely that he would appear concordant with Tim ("I'd say we act fairly similarly in those situations"), although in reality there might be important differences between them on these dimensions.

To illustrate this, there is considerable support for the view that Tim and Tom are discordant on important dimensions of sociability. For example, Tom describes more clearly his introversion in a later interview: "I guess I'm just shy around people, people say, 'you're shy,' and I mingle well with crowds, but as far as girls go I'm shy. I mean I don't force myself. I stay in the background. Like in junior high I'd go to a dance and be like a wallflower . . . my best friend in high school and junior high school was a wallflower too."

This is in marked contrast to what Tom says about Tim: "He's quite the wolf [laughs], like my boss at work. He and Tim go out together . . . I don't go with them . . . they go to [names a bar] and try to pick up women or dance."

There is some ambiguity in this account, since Tom says he is shy, yet he also says he mingles well with crowds. The focus of the discordance between these twins seems to center, in this excerpt, on relations with members of the opposite sex. However, Tim's description of junior high school suggests that the areas of discordance are somewhat broader:

"Our parents wanted [Tom] to get out, but . . . he just ended up staying home. [Parents tried to get Tim to include his twin in his social activities, but] I didn't want my brother tagging along with everything I did. That doesn't make us individuals and I guess that's what I wanted to be. I still . . . don't like my brother doing everything that I'm doing . . . not that he couldn't if he wanted to, but it's like him tagging along or something."

Earlier in this same interview Tim gave the following description of their social relationships: "My class [in junior high school] was very nice, and so many of the friends I met I kept all the way through [school]. Tom unfortunately didn't. . . . He made friends, but not a lot of real close friends like I did."

In this description, Tim's statements suggest that the points of dissimilarity on social dimensions may include the quantity of social activity that each of the twins engaged in, as well as the quality of social interaction, reflected in the maintenance of long-term relationships. Thus, Tim and Tom appear to be discordant for *both* the quantity and the quality dimension of sociability as described by Buss and Plomin (1975).

Stephanie and Melissa, twins in their mid-twenties, also seemed discordant both in quantity and quality of sociability. For example, Melissa described the following: "Stephanie is more of a social butterfly than I am, [she's] better at public relations than I am. She appears to be a little more relaxed at big social gatherings than I am; [it's] easier for her to make conversation. I'm more willing to sit back and watch."

Thus, these twins appear to be discordant in terms of quantity of sociability. However, it is also true for quality, as Melissa described in a later interview: "Stephanie's relationships don't last as long, but there's more of them. Mine are longer but not as frequent. . . . She tends to be more theatrical, has an expressive face when she talks, speaks loud, theatrical, maybe that puts people off [maybe that's why her relationships don't last as long]. She can talk and talk. Stephanie's a real social butterfly."

Cindy, from a third twinship, provides another illustration:

"Since we have been up here [at college], I've noticed differences in our personality, because if [Lindy] doesn't want to be bothered by someone, she's going to cut them off short. But if somebody comes up and talks to me, I might just put up with it and not say anything about it. But when people come up to me, guys might say, 'I heard you are kind of mean, you are kind of cold to people.' I say, 'That's not me.' And they say, 'It's one of you twins.' [And I say], 'Well, it must be my sister.' And there are quite a few people who say that she is quick tempered, and I am the one who will take time [with people]. I told [Lindy] about that, and I said, 'Why do you cut people off like that? People are coming up to me and telling me that they said something to me about it. They accuse me of cutting them off, and I didn't do that!' And she says, 'I didn't realize I was doing it.' 'Well, you do it,' I say. It seems like she does it a lot."

Similar differences were present in many of the MZ twins who participated in this study. Jean and Sandie were also quite different in terms of sociability. Sandie was described by both twins as considerably more sociable. She described herself as always "very giving of herself" to others. She had many friends, and Jean often felt left out of their activities, especially as they became adolescents. In Jean's perception, the twins had shared friends almost equally prior to adolescence; however, the change that transpired at that time was quite traumatic for Jean who reported the following incident:

"I remember this one really traumatic time I had. . . . I started yelling at Sandie, 'I just feel like a ping-pong ball because I don't know when I am part of your group and when I am not part of your group, and I don't even know when you are my friend, and I don't know when you are these other people's friend.' It was a really hard time." Sandie was considerably more popular than Jean.

Other examples could be mustered from twinships described below to illustrate apparent differences in sociability. The important point is that these differences, at least along some dimensions of sociability, appear significant. It is difficult to know their implication when juxtaposed with the studies reporting a strong genetic contribution to sociability. The problem may be definitional, or it may be that there are strong *undercurrents*, which these interviews do not tap. On the other hand, the various factors that might be grouped under the heading of sociability must refer to dimensions of everyday experience, if they have any meaning at all. Just what the relationship is between high concordance on the MMPI social introversion-extroversion scale and day-to-day twin behavior is unclear. For them to have any meaning, one needs to understand these connections. Thus, the descriptive material presented here does not necessarily dispute such findings, but it does suggest that MZ twins can be quite different on important social dimensions. Naturally, these differences would have environmental rather than genetic origins.

Dominance is a personality dimension that would appear to be important in an interpersonal sense and certainly related to sociability. Unlike sociability, studies that included measures of dominance have not found strong evidence of a genetic contribution. Gottesman (1963) found the heritability estimate for dominance to be zero on the MMPI Do scale. The same was not true for the HSPQ, which had a low heritability estimate of .31 for the total sample. But when he divided the sample by sex, Gottesman found marked differences between males and females in the heritability of dominance. On the MMPI a breakdown by sex revealed a heritability estimate of zero for females, while males had a low one (.33). The effects were more impressive for the HSPQ, where Gottesman again found virtually no genetic contribution to dominance for females but a great deal for males (H' = .74). In a later study using the CPI, Gottesman (1966) found evidence of a significant genetic contribution to dominance.

Dworkin et al. (1977) found dominance to have significant genetic variance in both adolescence and adulthood. In a later study of person-situation interactions, Dworkin (1979) administered a stimulus-response inventory of dominance to a group of twins. The subjects were asked to think of twelve specified situations (e.g., "You are in a theater-ticket line and someone pushes ahead.") and rate themselves on their likely reactions (i.e., "I say what's on my mind."). Dworkin found only weak support for a genetic contribution to dominance. As with Gottesman's study, Dworkin did find sex differences in his sample. Females' data provided evidence of sibling-environmental influences but no evidence of genetic variance. Males, on the other hand, provided "marginally significant evidence of genetic variance." But Dworkin's data for males revealed interesting differences when examined in terms of zygosity. DZ twins were actually more similar than MZ twins in their pattern of dominance across situations, while MZ twins were more similar in their total dominance score. Dworkin concluded that MZ twins are very similar in overall dominance but choose unrelated situations in which to express it.

Canter (1973), using the 16PF questionnaire, found intrapair twin correlations for assertiveness to be significant for *both* MZ and DZ twins. Judging from the illustration from Dworkin's inventory, it is reasonable to assume a close relationship between assertiveness and dominance. That both groups of twins showed significant correlations would suggest that this is an environmentally influenced trait. In fact, DZ twins actually had slightly higher correlations than MZ twins on this factor (.30 versus .27). On the other hand, the measure of tough-mindedness showed MZ correlations to be significantly higher than DZ correlations (.68 versus .25).

As was true to some extent with sociability, studies of the genetic contribution to dominance have varied in their results. Carter (1935),

Dworkin et al. (1977), Gottesman (1963, 1966), and Vandenberg (1966) would be examples of studies reporting at least some evidence for a genetic contribution to dominance. On the other hand, Canter (1973), Cattell, Blewitt, & Beleff (1955), Dworkin (1979), and Vandenberg (1962) have reported at least some results which suggest that the genetic contribution to dominance is at best weak. Differences in instrumentation, including questionnaires, make it difficult to assess accurately the implication of the varied results.

In the present study, many MZ subjects described interactions that clearly related to the construct of dominance (e.g., the extent to which one exerted control over another). Differences in dominance, conceived in these broad terms, were prevalent. With the male subjects, these differences were often manifested in terms of physical domination during childhood.

Charles, a twin in his early twenties, provided one clear illustration. He described an incident in which he knocked his brother Frank down while playing football. Frank got so aggravated "that of course he knocked me down, at the same time kicking me and things like that. I learned right then that it was to my best interest not to play football against him. And even when we were . . . older and out with the family, there were times that Frank and I could have been paired up against each other in blocking and running around, [but] I tended not to do it. To Frank it probably meant that I was afraid of him, and yes, I probably was a little bit, because I just didn't want the thing to go on further because I knew his capabilities. He's the type of person who needs to have himself on top at all times."

Later in the same interview Charles offered the following illustration of his brother's physical dominance:

"I remember one time he walked up to me in the hallway. This must have been our freshman year in high school . . . he walked up and just slugged the hell out of me. He walked up and said, 'You understand, don't you, that I have to show my friends that I can do that.' He walked away, and I thought, 'Wow, that's real mature.'. . . His big thing was hitting me that day. And me not responding, I think it made Frank realize immediately that I wasn't going to fight him. He was constantly trying to show his physical things to his other friends, about himself personally, and if they could drag me into it sometimes, so much the better."

A similar pattern was present with Tim and Tom. For example, early in his first interview Tom stated: "We learned long ago not to really fight."

Interviewer: "What do you mean?"

Tom: "We used to fist fight when we were young. Our older brother used to clear the furniture! I was always afraid to hit someone in the face or stomach or something, but Tim would get mad and hit me right in the mouth; he'd hit me in the stomach and in the mouth."

Interviewer: "How old were you?"

Tom: "About ten."

Interviewer: "What started these fights?"

Tom: "Anything. Who's going to sit in the front of the station wagon? . . . Tim has a hotter temper than I do. I'd slug him, but I wouldn't hit him on the face."

Dominance can have various manifestations, of course. There are other ways in which Tim's dominance shows up in this twinship. Most clearly it surfaces in the context of a number of arrangements in which Tom appears to be at a distinct disadvantage. For example, Tim is more conservative with his money and had managed to save a considerable sum for future graduate studies. Yet it seemed that, in a number of things that the twins discussed, Tom was saddled with a disproportionate amount of the expenses, regardless of the extent to which they might or might not benefit him. For example, the twins purchased a car "together," although Tom had paid for four-fifths of it as well as the insurance. However, Tim appeared to be the one who needed the car the most, since his girl friend lived twenty miles away (Tom's girl friend lived in the same apartment complex). Furthermore, when the twins went somewhere together in their car, it was Tim who inevitably drove, according to the twins. Similarly, the twins reported that they had given their mother a "joint" gift for Christmas, although Tom had contributed twice as much as Tim to the purchase price. Neither twin was quick to complain about these arrangements, although during one of the interviews, Tom did accuse Tim of being "Cheap! Cheap! Cheap!" when the matter of money came up.

While perhaps humorous in this instance, a consistent pattern of one twin getting his or her way more frequently than the other, or having his or her interests served more often, can be construed as an example of interpersonal dominance. Certainly the more overt illustrations of dominance, such as one twin being physically domineering over the other as in the earlier examples, become less and less likely with increasing age. Instead, social forms of dominance, rather than physical forms, must take their place. For example, no longer referring to physical control, Tom observed: "Tim is the more dominant of the two of us, I'm more the follower."

Stephanie and Melissa's relationship has similar characteristics. A trip to Europe less than a year before the interviews appears to have brought these differences out. For example, Stephanie described their reunion in Europe after she had already been there for a few months: "So when [Melissa] came over, there I was, proud as a peacock, 'I know my way around here. I'm going to show you.' So I took care of all of the money matters, all the planning of where we would go, deciding where we could go, how, when we would go, because I knew my way around."

Stephanie went on to describe a major point of conflict during the trip regarding whether they should go to Greece or Spain:

"I wanted to go to Greece, she, Spain, like two opposing poles . . . so we went to Greece instead of France and Spain. [But] she did get her way [said humorously]. We did go to France for two hours. She got her croissants, [laughs] so it all worked out. It was amazing because we just knew where we wanted to go. We both wanted to go to the same places. . . . I took care of the money matters, worked out the finances, and I just liked working out the travel plans. I *have* to be in charge of things, to know what is happening. I'm not a follower when it comes down to traveling!"

At a later juncture in this same interview, in describing the twins' use of their car, Stephanie noted that "Melissa tends to drive. I give directions."

The dimension of dominance, at least as reflected in Stephanie's taking command of their European trip and local travel, appears to be discordant in this twinship. Interestingly, it seemed that this feature of their relationship was currently in a state of transformation. For example, Melissa also talked about their trip to Europe in similar terms; however, it seemed clear that since her return, she had begun to examine the implications of these characteristics of her relationship with Stephanie. She noted that she felt somewhat insecure in general and that something about their return from Europe had made her begin to question that. At first this was depicted as something that both she and Stephanie felt:

"Coming home and falling into a childish period and not having to think on your own—we felt that coming back from Europe. Even though I did the following, you could *not* have two leaders in Europe, so one had to be the leader, and one had to be the follower, but we were both adults."

Immediately after this statement, though, Melissa made it clear that these feelings had a great deal to do with Stephanie, as she described her decision to accept a friend's invitation to move in as a roommate, which meant leaving Stephanie behind living at home: "I just got tired, wanted to be on my own. And I found myself relying on [Stephanie] too much. She was making decisions for me and stuff, and I really felt bad about the whole thing."

Later in this same interview she described the feeling of wanting to be by herself sometimes and wanting to be self-sufficient: "There was a time [before she moved out of her parents' home] when I was very unhappy. I had security with [name of boyfriend], being with Stephanie, being at home, but I was never really the leader, never really in charge of *myself*."

One final example will serve to illustrate possible discordance for dominance in a pair of identical twins. The interviewer observed that one twin, Valery, had done most of the talking for both during the joint interview and asked, "Is that a pattern between you?"

Vickie responded, "No, it really isn't. It just depends. The way it was was she just started talking, and I didn't want to interrupt. This is the way it is sometimes . . . she started talking, and she likes to run things. She was doing a good job, so I just let her talk . . . sometimes I won't let her [run things], but if it doesn't bother me, I will let her. There was one time—we used to always fight over who drove because she wanted to drive more than I did, or she was trying to drive more. We used to have this deal where she would drive up [to home town], and I would drive back. It usually worked out, but sometimes we would forget. Most of the time it was just that she wanted to drive more, and finally it's clear that she drives most of the time, always. She was trying to take it over and finally I gave in."

In a later interview Vickie was more to the point: "A lot of times [Valery] is, she's overpowering. She bosses me more . . . she does boss me around sometimes."

Like Tim and Tom, Vickie and Valery had occasional fistfights as children. Vickie explained, "Sometimes we would get in fistfights. If I didn't quit, she wouldn't. It was like she always had to have the last punch, which I didn't care. I didn't want to hit anymore, so I stopped. But I got tired of it sometimes. There used to be a time when I wouldn't do anything, I would give in and say, 'Forget it.' Nowadays I still don't like her to boss me around too much."

Like Tim and Tom, early physical dominance seems to have been replaced by more subtle interactions. As evidenced by the differences over driving their car, it appears that Vickie still acquiesces to Valery.

In the fourth interview Vickie spontaneously brought up Valery's control of the joint interview: "I would love it if she would give in, but very rarely does that happen. Sometimes it doesn't bother me. In the interview the very first day it didn't bother me that she was talking . . . but like the car bit. Like if it was my turn to drive and she would get into the seat, I would want to drive and I didn't want to give in. So we would both be so stubborn. She would be sitting in the driver's seat, and I would be standing by the door, repeatedly asking her to get out. Sometimes we would end up getting into a fight, but if not, we would just end up sitting there for the longest time—like for thirty minutes—because we both wouldn't want to give in. So, finally, I would be tired of standing, so I would go around and get in the other seat. I would be furious all the way home. . . . This really used to make me mad, but after a while I just didn't want to stand there anymore. A lot of times when we would fight, the fight would go on forever if I didn't let her have the last word or whatever. It's not that bad anymore. Like I said, nowadays I don't mind that much, I don't drive that much anymore."

Clearly, the interview material which has been presented thus far cannot be considered a definitive critique of the genetic research on dominance or sociability. However, this material does contain a degree of face validity with respect to these constructs that is not easily dismissed. These interviews suggest that there may be important differences between MZ twins that need to be considered carefully when assessing genetic contributions to personality development. It is difficult to appreciate fully the differences between identical twins without looking at their lives in greater detail. In the remainder of the chapter, several case studies will be presented to illustrate how extensive some of the differences between MZ twins can be. The relevance of such an approach to the thesis of this book is obvious: the greater the environmental contribution to personality organization, the more important it is to examine carefully the developmental context of twinship itself for factors that might account for the differences observed.

Twins who have been separated early in life would be expected to show the greatest disparity on dimensions related to environment and experience, especially if their environments were markedly dissimilar. At the same time, such twins would be expected to maintain considerable similarity in those factors having a major genetic contribution. One of the cases in Newman et al. (1937) of twins who were reared apart provides an excellent illustration of both of these aspects. Gladys and Helen were MZ twins separated at approximately eighteen months of age. They were not reunited until they were twenty-eight years old. Each twin was adopted into a family that differed from the other in important ways.

Their adoption histories, for example, were somewhat different. Gladys had been adopted by a Canadian family living in a small Ontario community. Her adoptive father worked for the railroad. Helen, on the other hand, was adopted from the same orphanage by adoptive parents who were far from ideal. The father is described as being an "unstable character," while Helen's first adoptive mother is reported to have become insane two years after Helen was adopted into their home. Helen was then returned to the same orphanage where, after several months, she was adopted by a farmer and his wife. Helen was raised on a farm in Michigan, where she lived until she was twenty-five, with the exception of four years spent at college. Newman et al. make the observation that although Helen and Gladys were brought up in different countries, in fact, "culturally there is no great difference between Ontario and Michigan . . . on the whole, Ontario is somewhat more conservative than Michigan, and the population of Ontario is somewhat more homogeneous than that of Michigan; but it does not seem to us that the contrast is very great" (p. 247). In addition, both twins, having married, ended up living in Detroit—Helen for eight years, Gladys for ten years—at the time that they participated in the Newman study.

During the time she would have been attending the fourth and fifth grades, Gladys lived in a secluded town in the Canadian Rockies where there were no educational opportunities available to her. The authors report that by the time Gladys moved back to Ontario, she was "probably too old to associate comfortably with third-graders." Whether for this reason or another, Gladys never returned to school, resulting in nearly a total lack of formal education. Helen, on the other hand, had a very different experience. Despite her adoptive father's opinion that higher education for women was nonsense, Helen's adoptive mother was determined that Helen should have every educational opportunity. As a result, Helen was never really required to work on the family's farm and was permitted, instead, to devote herself to her studies. Helen graduated from a good college and became a teacher. In terms of education, these twins could not have been more different.

Newman et al. note that on the whole the physical differences between the twins were small relative to the mental and temperamental differences. "What differences are present seem to be correlated with the great difference in the lives of the two women, for they are mainly associated with differences in carriage of body and facial expression—differences obviously acquired in the course of their different social activities" (p. 249).

These twins differed markedly on the various tests of ability administered by the researchers. Helen surpassed Gladys on every test of ability. For example, in the Stanford-Binet the difference between the twins was three years and ten months, or twenty-four points in IQ. Newman et al. note that this difference was "nearly five times as great as the mean difference between identical twins reared together and nearly three times as great as the mean difference between the nineteen [reared apart MZ] pairs." Helen's score was quite high, with Gladys's score falling sixty-nine percentile points below Helen's (i.e., 69 percent of the scores of the general population would lie between their two scores).

As a teacher, Helen taught a variety of courses but principally concentrated on English and history. Gladys, on the other hand, was "needed at home for housework" and had no other occupation until she was seventeen, at which time she went to work in a knitting mill. When Gladys moved to Detroit, she eventually went to work in a printing office, setting type, copywriting, and proofreading. Newman et al. note that the latter activities "must be regarded as having some educational value." Nevertheless, the twins differed markedly in their performance on tests measuring language-related activities. Even though Gladys used language skills in her vocation of proofreading, Helen was superior by two years and six months in spelling, and one year and eight months in language.

This set of twins may be seen as illustrating Gottesman's (1963) point that heredity fixes a reaction range which is subject to environmental influences. In this case, it is possible that each of these twins had an innate talent in the verbal sphere. Both can be seen as having overcome considerable adversity. For an individual who had only a third-grade education, Gladys would have seemed unlikely to be a proofreader. Similarly, Helen, like Gladys, apparently had an early childhood that was quite chaotic, living in an orphanage until she was eighteen months, but then spending the next two and a half years under very difficult circumstances prior to being adopted by her second adoptive parents. Even here, however, Helen's environment, in spite of her adoptive mother's interest in Helen's education, could not be considered as highly conducive to a college education in the 1920s. Her adoptive mother had had no education, and her adoptive father was not supportive of Helen's education. Finally, Helen grew up on a farm rather than in an urban environment where greater access to educational opportunities would have been likely.

Thus, if anything, one commonality in Helen's and Gladys's backgrounds was that in neither case was the environment readily supportive of vocational aspirations that were verbal. Nevertheless, both twins established themselves in highly verbal careers. It is likely, then, that this inclination toward the verbal sphere is part of the (hereditary) reaction range with which both were endowed, to use Gottesman's phrase. However, as Gottesman further notes, within this reaction range, environment may serve to accentuate or inhibit the unfolding of the genetically given propensity. In this case, although both twins were verbally oriented, Helen's actual attainment far surpassed that of Gladys.

The differences in the personalities of these twins, as reported by Newman and his colleagues, were even more striking, as evidenced by the following quotation:

Observations of the overt behavior of these twins revealed some further important personality differences. Helen is a confident and suave person with rather marked charm of manner. She makes the most of her personal appearance, moves about gracefully, and is apparently conscious of making a favorable impression on men. She conversed smoothly without a trace of diffidence and always took the lead in all matters pertaining to arrangements for the trip and the stay in Chicago. One sees at once that she is by far the more aggressive in her overt acts, but the Downey test revealed about equally strong aggressiveness in the two women. Gladys made the impression upon us of a person ill at ease. This attitude may have been partly the result of a feeling of inferiority in view of the apparent certainty that she would make a comparatively poor showing on the tests. She seemed to us to be a rather staid and stolid person, distinctly diffident. She had no affectations to match those of her sister and had no charm of manner or grace of movement. She was not becomingly dressed nor did she make the best of her physique. She never volunteered any information and was difficult to draw into conversation. She made no effort to create a favorable personal impression. In general, the contrast in overt behavior during social contacts was rather extreme (pp. 249–250).

It is clear that Helen and Gladys impressed the researchers with the extent of their personal differences. Interestingly, however, these differences were not as marked in their performance on personality tests. Nevertheless, the authors note, "While the differences in personality are not so clearly and simply shown in the tests as are the differences in ability, it can scarcely be doubted that differences of both kinds do exist in rather marked degree and that they have been produced by the environment. This inference is drawn from the fact that differences between the sisters and between their environment are both very large and the further fact that the differences between the twins are in the direction we should expect them to be from the nature of the environmental differences" (p. 255).

The differences that Newman et al. described were generalized and ingrained, rather than transient or situational. In other words, there were significant differences in personality between these twins, differences which are most easily explained in terms of dissimilarities in their environment. Yet a common assumption of twin research is that MZ twins who are not reared apart share a comparable environment.

By turning now to some illustrations of MZ twins who were raised together, we will see two important features of the twin situation: First, despite their genetic similarity, identical twins reared together are, in fact, quite different. Second, the assumption of equal environments, at least when examined in this more detailed manner, has important limitations since the best explanation of differences between these MZ twins is that there are within-family factors, including the twin situation itself, which are at work in shaping varying personality characteristics.

Twin subjects in this study participated in intensive, semistructured interviews that altogether totaled two to six hours. Often, in these interviews, I was struck by the polarization of personality characteristics in MZ twinships. It is a paradox of twinship that many of the subjects who, on the one hand, appeared to mirror each other to a great extent in that they are remarkably alike (psychologically), simultaneously appeared to be quite different in many other respects. There seemed to be a rather fortuitous or arbitrary division of personality characteristics, which appeared to be a caricature of social roles, a caricature of opposites. It is possible that this polarization has a clear-cut function, creating as it does areas of expertise or domains of selfhood, through which twins achieve a nonconflictual sense of themselves as different and unique. This radical dichotomy may have its value, then, in that it becomes the mooring of a "self-system," and it is around these distinguishing characteristics that each twin's sense of self as separate from the co-twin becomes organized.

The extent to which each twin subscribed to a similar depiction of his or her characteristics and those of the twin was remarkable in its consistency, especially during the course of separate interviews. Cindy and Lindy provide one vivid example of this phenomenon. In their interviews, these eighteen-year-old twins both described Lindy as "the outgoing one," she was the "adventurous one," the "aggressive one." Cindy, on the other hand, was routinely characterized as the "homebody type," "in a shell," "quiet one," and generally shy and reserved. These characterizations were reflected in their activities as well. While Lindy had a job in high school, Cindy preferred to stay home. Lindy enjoyed frequent dates on weeknights as well as on weekends; Cindy stayed home, enjoyed cooking, and did the twins' homework. She was described by both of them as "the maternal one." These disparities were not as consistent as the initial depictions, though. For instance, "adventurous" Lindy gave up an opportunity to go to Europe because it would have meant going without Cindy. Cindy, on the other hand, was actively making plans to enroll in the junior-year-abroad program at her university. Nevertheless, the twins were remarkably consistent in the descriptions they presented of themselves and each other.

Tim and Tom have already been discussed in terms of sociability and dominance. These twins also gave consistent descriptions of themselves. Both twins described Tim as the "adventurous one," the "aggressive one." If they went to a garage sale, Tom would be more likely to select an item for purchase. It would then be left up to Tim to dicker about the price. Tom was more domestically inclined, enjoyed cooking, and was more preoccupied with keeping their apartment orderly and clean. Even activities in which both twins seemed to share an interest at times reflected important differences in approach. For example, Tim was interested in artwork as a source of investment, whereas Tom's interest was predominantly aesthetic. Although both twins had participated in high school athletics, Tim was decidedly more athletic.

It is true that the twinships just described are similar in ways that are also quite striking. For example, Cindy and Lindy had slept in the same bed until college. They continued to live in the same dormitory but were not sharing a room, as they had requested, only because of an administrative mix-up. They shared the same best friend, were rushed by the same sorority, and took many of the same classes. Tim and Tom shared an apartment and worked at the same facility, doing the same kind of work and making the same salary. There was a tremendous degree of overt similarity in these two twinships, and they appeared to enjoy it. Because they did not try to minimize their twinness, such efforts cannot account for the degree of dissimilarity to be found in these twinships along the dimensions I have described. In many twinships, powerful developmental forces may encourage similarity on some dimensions while encouraging dissimilarity on others. Further, we are accustomed to think of differences between twins as being environmentally generated while the similarities are often thought to be genetic. This is only partially true. It is likely that at least *some* of the similarities between MZ twins are also attributable to their environment as Plomin and Rowe (1979) found.

Let us examine more closely the twinship of Jean and Sandie. Although these twins, in their early twenties, were not, as Sandie put it, "the kinds of twins that did everything together," nevertheless, they have many features in common with the twins that have already been described.

As infants they looked so much alike that their mother had to use colored pins to identify them. The twins dressed alike until fifth grade and continued to do so on special occasions until their thirteenth birthday. Twinness was emphasized in other ways as well. For example, in elementary school the twins went to a Halloween party dressed as a two-headed monster. Other years they went dressed as toothbrush and toothpaste, and the King and Queen of Hearts. As is not unusual among identical twins, Sandie and Jean, prompted by their schoolmates, switched places in school on one occasion—a prank which was temporarily successful. The twins look sufficiently alike that others still frequently confuse them.

The twins were quite similar in other ways as well. As children they were often sick at the same time. Both had their tonsils out together ("I remember coming home, we had matching stuffed animals, eating the same thing, and everything was fine"—Sandie). Both had to have twelve teeth extracted at the same time ("We both went under at the same time. . . . We did it next to each other, so we could see each other . . . it makes it easier if someone else is going through the same thing."—Sandie). As adolescents, both twins had problems with scoliosis, a congenital condition, although Sandie's was more pronounced and required that she wear a back brace for two years.

Academically, both twins did very well. Their grade point averages were almost the same (Jean's was 4.0, Sandie's 3.96). The twins shared a "best student award" in elementary school. Both twins won scholarships that came from their elementary school. Throughout their school years Sandie and Jean were "pretty much always in the top of the class."

Along with the many striking similarities in this twinship are a number of differences that are equally impressive and consistent. For example, Jean was ten ounces heavier than Sandie at birth. This weight difference has always been a distinguishing feature. As adults, Jean is also two inches taller than Sandie (the persistence of such differences in MZ twins has been reported by others, e.g., Babson & Phillips, 1973). Moreover, Jean has always been somewhat more advanced than Sandie in terms of motor development. Jean apparently learned how to get out of the twins' crib first. On one occasion their mother is reported to have found Jean "lifting [Sandie's] foot over the crib to show her how to climb out too." These differences persisted. Jean described herself as always more athletically inclined than Sandie. Unlike Sandie, Jean was always involved in sports throughout her school years. In discussing some of their dissimilarities, Jean noted that in junior high school she had given Sandie some lessons in basketball so that "the other kids wouldn't laugh at her"; in return, Sandie had helped Jean with her writing.

During infancy, the twins differed somewhat in frustration tolerance, at least as reflected in their behavior while eating. For example, Sandie reported: "One of the first things that [mother] had trouble with was that she couldn't feed us at exactly the same time. There was no way for her to work it out. So at first she would alternate who got fed first, but my sister would always complain if I got fed first. I would be quiet if Jean got fed first, so she just ended up feeding her first and me second. So we have all these pictures of my sister being fed and me just looking." Burlingham (1952) also noted similar differences in eating patterns for some of the MZ twins at the Hampstead Clinic.

Other important differences between the twins became apparent from fairly early in their development. Lytton (1980) reported that some of his twin subjects appeared to divide the parents as objects of attachment, with one twin being more closely allied with the mother and the other with the father. Burlingham (1952) reported similar observations. Such divisions form the basis for subsequent identifications (A. Freud, 1981), and the consequences of such differential attachments are most apparent in these twinships. This appeared to be the case with Jean and Sandie. Sandie was considerably more interested in stereotypically female activities as a child, such as playing with dolls, whereas Jean was not the least bit interested in this sort of activity according to the twins. Instead, Jean was more inclined toward playing "Man from U.N.C.L.E." When possible, Jean accompanied her father to play golf, an activity in which Sandie was not interested. Both twins described Jean as a tomboy during the elementary school years. It may be that Jean's being physically more robust than Sandie contributed in an important way to this differential pattern of identification.

If we consider these differences as related to sex-role identification, then they may also be related to important contrasts in the twins' academic achievement. As noted earlier, the difference in their grade point averages was negligible; however, the twins reported important divergences in their areas of interest. Sandie was particularly strong in literature and art. Jean, on the other hand, was strong in courses related to mathematics and science. According to the twins, these variations in emphasis were already present in elementary school. A concise representation of possible differences in stereotypic sex-role identification between Sandie and Jean is found in their political careers in elementary school. In the same election Sandie ran for secretary of the student council, whereas Jean ran for the presidency.

These divergences had remained consistent into adulthood. In college, Sandie was a liberal arts major; Jean had received a bachelor's degree in a scientific area and was attending graduate school in a science-related field. On closer examination the apparent similarity of their grade point averages reveals considerable differences that bear a resemblance to sex-role identifications insofar as the usual sex-role stereotype for maleness is associated with greater athletic activity and with mathematics and science in terms of academic involvement.

Lytton (1980), Cohen et al. (1972), Plomin and Rowe (1979) and others have reported that in their studies parents of MZ twins have been able to detect minute differences in their twins. At times, according to Cohen et al., these differences are exaggerated and magnified, perhaps as a way of facilitating a differentiation between the twins. This was the case for Sandie and Jean. In reference to the miniscule differences in their grades, Sandie reports that she was termed "the dumb one," despite a 3.96 grade point average. It appears that Sandie internalized these perceptions of herself to some extent. She said at one point in reference to the small margin of difference in the twins' grades: "That margin, it was small, so small that it *should be* insignificant, but you start believing it yourself." During another interview, Sandie returned to this same point and said: "In terms of myself, I don't feel *inadequate*. But after a while you feel it without even wanting to feel it or believe it."

In school the twins' teachers also appeared to be quite aware of these points of divergence. According to Sandie, these differences were sometimes "used as a tool." She described a teacher in elementary school saying to her, "'You and your sister have the same IQ, so why are you getting a D in math? You score almost as high on math achievement, so why are you doing so poorly?'" Sandie's response was that there were other things that she was interested in, things in which she performed better than Jean, such as English and history.

Another indication that these differences did become a primary vehicle for differentiating the twins is reflected in the following comment by Sandie: "A few times we attempted to switch classes, but they *always* knew . . . they never knew that Jean wasn't me, but they knew that I wasn't Jean. Because Jean has a flair for math and science, they would say, 'You can't be Jean, Jean would have had that question right.'" Note that in this report it is not physical differences that form the basis for the teacher's inference that it was "the wrong twin," rather, it was a difference in a "flair for math and science."

These points of divergence, as the comment suggests, appeared to become reflected as slight differences in achievement, minor differences that were subsequently accentuated. For example, Jean noted that although the twins shared an achievement award from their Sunday school, a friend of hers claimed to have seen the original list of names in order of achievement. She reported that Jean's name had been first on the list, Sandie's third. For reasons that are unclear, though no doubt because Jean and Sandie were twins, they had been given a second-place award to share, while another child was given the "valedictorian" award. Jean felt this to be unfair. Similarly, Jean won a National Merit Scholarship upon graduation from high school, while Sandie won a language award, considered less prestigious. It is difficult to tell whether these differences in achievement reflect minor differences in potential or whether they reflect differences in socialization and perception. From a genetic point of view one would not expect the dissimilarities to be a function of different endowment since they are MZ twins. Rather, it seems more likely that these divergences reflect differential identification with the parents, subtle differences in perception and expectation on the part of the parents, or other environmental influences. Nevertheless, it is clear that minor divergences in this twinship became magnified in the course of their development.

In spite of many similarities, the striking differences between them on a number of important dimensions appear to have had a more important impact on their lives. Even in arenas where, overtly, some of the divergences were minimal, as in their actual achievement in school, these tiny differences appear to have been magnified and transformed into dissimilarities that had some consequence in terms of how each twin felt about herself.

Henri and Ian form another twinship that reflects considerable differences. In their late forties, the twins continue to look remarkably alike. In photographs, both as children and adults, Henri and Ian are indistinguishable. Even as adults they have occasionally played identity tricks on others. For example, one summer, during a visit to the city where Ian lives, Henri, alone at a concert, was "recognized" as Ian by one of Ian's friends. Henri carried on a conversation with this "friend" for several minutes before telling him that he was not Ian, but Ian's twin brother. The friend was incredulous, and Henri had to muster considerable evidence to convince him that he was not Ian.

Henri and Ian's voices sound alike on tape recordings. More striking is the similarity in their lives. The twins were in the same classes from elementary school through college. Only in their last semester of college did they take a few different courses, although they did not actually have the same major. They participated in plays together in college. When growing up, they often dressed alike, which their mother preferred. This was true well into college:

Henri: "Even up until we graduated from college, we had never bought a different suit. We always bought the same suit; most of our basic clothes were the same. Sometimes we would wear different clothes, but we had the same. We looked very much alike. Most people couldn't tell us apart."

After college, Henri and Ian spent many years as priests in the same

Catholic order, having entered one year apart. When they were in their early forties, Ian left the order to get married. Henri left the order three years later. Both twins teach on college campuses. Thus the lives of Henri and Ian converge to a considerable degree; however, the differences in their lives are also evident. As with other twinships, Henri and Ian appear to have differed somewhat in sociability, as Henri confirmed: "I became more introspective, was identified as 'the quiet one,' a little less outgoing, not identified as real morose, but, I guess I was less talkative. I definitely had more moods than my brother seemed to have."

Ian, on the other hand, is described as more outgoing and extroverted, as reflected in the following material from their joint interview:

Henri: "I think Ian probably is more of a natural, enjoys performance more. We were always performing. We were constantly going out, [or] relatives were coming over, and it was always, 'Oh isn't it wonderful, identical twins, now do something for us,' 'recite poems,' 'dance,' 'say something,' 'be cute.' I think I enjoyed that less than Ian. I was more introverted than Ian . . . I remember I never liked to argue, have big discussions, debates, and things like that. I remember with Uncle D., when he'd come over you [Ian] and [brother] or someone might be arguing or talking about something, and Ian seemed to enjoy that. I would rather be off reading a book, and I remember thinking, 'Ian really likes that and I really don't.'"

Later in the same interview Ian summed up these differences with the following statement: "I suppose I would say that Henri was the quiet twin. I was the talkative twin."

Although Ian is described as the more sociable, outgoing twin, both twins view Henri as having been more interested in girls since elementary school and as always having had more girl friends. This was a family joke.

Ian described another difference between the twins: "I remember another distinction, and I chuckle about this. It probably is a real character line between us. When we went to Europe in 1950, mother had given both of us these diaries, and I remember . . . mine was full of poetry, just poetry, and Henri's had things like 'today we got up at eight and had breakfast.' Mine's poetry and Henri's is prose [laughs], there it was . . ." Henri breaks in: "Details, I was into details."

In another interview Henri described the differences in character in the following terms: "When Ian's around, you just give up because he's just going to talk and not listen to anybody, to jabber away. Maybe he talked a little more than I did, a little more nervous. In grade school he did talk more than I did. I was identified as the quieter of the two of us."

Henri described their seminary experience in similar terms. For example, in Henri's view, Ian enjoyed the seminary in part because of "the camaraderie of the community . . . it was just the opposite for me, I liked the studies more. I don't think I was considered a recluse, [but] I didn't feel that close to anybody."

As with other twinships described here, some of the dissimilarities between Henri and Ian appear to be linked to differential relationships with the parents. The twins' mother was of French-American descent, while their father was Irish-American. The twins' names obviously reflected the differing parental backgrounds. Henri was repeatedly referred to as "the French twin" while Ian was "the Irish twin." This had been the case during their childhood as well. Henri spontaneously made the observation that some of the differences between himself and Ian were linked to this differing cultural emphasis.

One of the most divergent MZ twinships in this study was that of Charles and Frank. These twins were in their early twenties. Only Charles was interviewed because Frank lives in another city. The dimensions in which they differed were many and quite marked. For example, the twins were discordant for homosexuality.[1] Differences between Charles and Frank in dominance have already been described. They also differed considerably in sociability, with Frank consistently described as being markedly antisocial, including a long history of destruction of others' belongings and general lack of consideration for others. Charles, in contrast, described himself as interested in people, often having parties for others in high school.

Charles cited the following incident in a motel swimming pool when they were nine or ten years old as illustrative of these differences:

"My brother was the macho one who was constantly trying to see how much water he could get on the people who were trying to enjoy

[1] The twin literature contains other illustrations of MZ twins discordant for homosexuality (e.g., Zuger, 1976).

the pool, and I was trying to swim because I was always the swimmer. . . . Frank spent a lot of time really being antagonistic, I think. I tried to be nice to people—at times I think I was more conscious of the fact that since I looked so much like him, that I wanted to make myself really different so people would notice that I'm not as much the ass that he is."

These differences were manifested in a number of ways. Frank was actively involved with sports. Charles remembers a coach being disappointed that he was not playing football. The coach assumed that because Frank was such a capable football player that Charles must be good as well. According to Charles, however, "I couldn't throw a football if I had to then."

Regarding their differing interests in athletics: "I took baton lessons [one] year [when I was twelve years old]. That was because I saw the guy who did the baton at the football games. I enjoyed halftime much more than the football. Frank watched the football, and I watched halftime."

Charles is unusually articulate and vivid in his descriptions of the differences in the twinship: "The older we got the further apart we got. That's just because each of us chose different roads. I don't drink, just as a rule. I was always seen as going to clubs and things like that because I enjoyed the environment, to me it was a very mature environment. When you're sixteen or seventeen, you can get into private clubs. Well, my brother took advantage of that more by going there and becoming inebriated—and seeing him do it, it sort of told me more not to do it. It was like, 'Frank is drinking and I should just let *him* drink.'"

Again regarding their drinking habits: "I don't drink beer, my friends drink expensive liqueurs, and I can't afford it all the time, but I'm real big on sending thank-you notes when I go to cocktail parties and things like that. To Frank, he'd never even want to go to a cocktail party. To him, he'd just as soon spend $2.50 on a six-pack, get in his pickup truck, and ride out to the lake and drink beer."

"[Frank's] group [in high school] were real hell raisers [describes Frank as spending his time on activities such as driving in circles on football fields, driving through people's fields and yards in his pickup truck], and my group was really active in student government and brotherhood and things like that." Charles was president of the student government in high school.

Regarding adolescent play: "My friends would want to go out and [water] ski and have a nice time. Frank wanted to go out—his big thing was to see how close he could get to another boat without actually hitting it, but scaring the other driver or a skier."

In describing their high school graduation ceremony: "When they called our names, I graduated with honors. When they called Frank, he stood up, and I don't think he was even wearing pants under his robe, long hair, maybe he had shaved, I'm not sure. He just kind of sauntered up there and swung the diploma around. Just really didn't give a hoot. And there I came up, and I had a suit underneath my robe, very clean-cut and shaven, tanned, because it was at the end of the year. And I had honor cords because I graduated with honors. I remember a lot of people coming up and telling me, 'It was strange to see how your brother and you have just different ways of walking.'" Frank went to a little-known agricultural college where he flunked out. Charles, in contrast, attended a prestigious university in his state.

Charles described himself as follows: "I have certain tastes I've acquired that I will not give up. I eat only Hägen-Dazs ice cream, and not just because it's popular, but because it's good for you. . . . I see a lot of movies and I buy a lot of books to read. I don't have a TV. I iron my own clothes. I'm real picky about what I want to wear. I like the preppy stuff that comes out; it's well made and it's going to last a long time."

In contrast, Charles described Frank as follows: "Frank is bearded . . . has sort of the cowboy beard, his is the rustic look. Look in the back of *Alpine Trail* or at an article in the paper about logging in Canada or Alaska, that's the sort of look that Frank has. He always wears holey blue jeans, the seat and the knees are always worn out, old cowboy boots or old logger boots, flannel shirt—always that type. Sometimes it's a flannel shirt with long johns underneath; if it's real cold, he'll slip a goose-down jacket over it. That's just how Frank is. Sometimes there's a blade of grass in his mouth—just real rustic looking."

From an early age Charles was musically inclined. Frank was not. Charles was considerably more domestic: "It turns out that I can cook fairly well, and he has a hard time putting TV dinners in the oven."

Charles described their differences: "I'm a big-city person at times, whereas Frank can live in [names small rural town where Frank lives]." Charles went on to describe his fantasies of living in New York or Washington, D.C., and having Frank come to visit, showing him the big city.

Finally, regarding their room decorations in adolescence: "Frank started collecting posters of rock stars and violent things up until . . . just recently. [Recalling when they started collecting posters around age twelve], I remember having a *Love Story* poster up on the wall, and I started having more softer things, more pleasant posters. So when we were sharing rooms, half of the room is this black light, really heavy into rock 'n' roll, and the other half was 'come to the fields,' springtimey things. That was a big change, because people would say, 'Well, I can always tell Charles's side of the room.' Whereas, my bed was always made, his never was. Mother always had to constantly remind him. . . . I still make my bed to this day, but Frank never did."

Unlike Henri and Ian, MZ twins whose lives were exceedingly parallel, Charles's and Frank's lives were marked by contrasts in nearly every facet. Because Charles was so articulate in depicting the differences between himself and his twin brother in vivid terms, one can readily see that the differences he described are major in behavioral manifestations and world view. They permit one to see in relief that personality variables can be quite discordant in MZ twins. By looking more closely at these differences, it is possible to see with greater clarity that there are dimensions of functioning on which MZ twins differ that appear to be significant and readily identifiable. It is possible, however, that they are not as easily identifiable in the context of objective tests, especially since the particulars of these important differences appear to vary from twinship to twinship.

It should be kept in mind that the purpose of the present work is not to examine thoroughly the question of genetic contribution to personality development. Twinship, to the extent that it constitutes a particular developmental situation that affects personality development, has implications for discussions of genetic versus environmental contributions to personality. It also has implications for the assumption that twins share essentially equal environments—a prevalent and important assumption for the Twin Method. If MZ twins are as different as these interviews suggest, questions are raised regarding the status of traditional approaches to twin research. Newman and colleagues, in their 1937 study, took a comprehensive approach to twinship, which included extensive psychometric assessments with objective tests as well as in-depth case-studies. Later genetic researchers have tended to limit themselves to the use of objective instruments and procedures. Although the interest in a scientifically sound approach is laudable, the danger inherent in the latter approach is a loss of real contact with the phenomena under consideration. As the material in this chapter illustrates, lurking beneath similar responses to a questionnaire may be major differences in experience, perception, and mode of interaction.

3

The Psychological Development of Twins

Identity formation is often considered the cornerstone of any discussion of the psychology of twinship. The idea that twins encounter difficulties in the process of identity formation is as pervasive in scientific writings on twinship as it is in popular culture. What does it mean, specifically, to say that twins encounter difficulties in identity formation? This is an overarching term that covers a great variety of psychological phenomena. As yet there is no systematic theoretical framework for understanding this and other important dimensions of the psychological development of twins. Further, the partial explanations in the literature on twins are for the most part inadequate.

In this chapter I present a theoretical framework for understanding the complications in twin identity formation and their psychological development more generally. I draw heavily from a variety of developmental theorists, with special attention to separation-individuation theory and the work of Mahler and her colleagues (1963, 1968, 1972; Mahler, Pine, & Bergman, 1975). The aim is to provide an underlying conceptualization of twin development as well as to indicate the developmental junctures at which twin development may be unusually stressed.

It is my view that twinship constitutes a specific developmental context that has specific implications for personality development. Further, this developmental context may yield characteristic psychological features. However, I believe this context to be specific rather than unique. In other words, I am not suggesting that the psychology of twinship is necessarily or fundamentally different from the psychological experience of the nontwin. In fact, many of the psychological features seen in twins can also be found in singletons, reflected in such phenomena as "twinning reactions" (Joseph & Tabor, 1961) and seen with siblings who are very close in age (Deutsch, 1938; Joseph & Tabor, 1961). The aim here is not to establish a separate psychology of twinship but rather to place a psychology of twinship firmly in the context of developmental theory.

It is necessary to draw a distinction between the characteristic psychological features of twin development and psychopathological organizations associated with major stresses in development, particularly in the separation-individuation process. This is an especially important distinction given that separation-individuation theory now occupies a prominent place in the conceptualization of psychological development and organization, with obstruction in the separation-individuation process often thought to indicate a pathogenic factor. This chapter offers a description of the development of individuals whose early psychological environment has been somewhat altered. Hence, we may see heightened manifestations of issues associated with separation-individuation in twin development, although these may not be pathological. It is indispensable that the reader keep in mind Hartmann's (1958) conceptualizations that suggest that one of the foremost functions of the ego is to adapt to the conditions presented by one's environment. The ego is thus colored by the characteristics of the environment by virtue of its adaptation to it.

An analogy may clarify the distinction between a personality organization that bears the mark of a particular developmental process as an ego adaptation and one in which symptoms are formed as a result of overwhelming stress. The only child, for example, has been the subject of considerable folklore as well as scientific research, just as twins have. One of the common conclusions of this research has been that growing up as an only child often results in particular psychological characteristics (for a full discussion see Falbo, 1982). One might say that the personality organization of the single child bears the mark of growing up within that specific developmental context. However, the fact that developmental circumstances may give an identifiable cast to personality organization does not necessarily bear on the question of adequacy of adaptation. In the final analysis, extent of developmental interference, quality of adaptation, and effectiveness of function are the arbiters between normal and pathological adjustment.

These points are especially important in approaching the psychol-

ogy of twinship; for what little knowledge is available on the psychological characteristics of twinship has often been derived from clinical
contexts. Although this work has been extremely informative, it
tends to place the discussion of twin psychology within a pathological
framework—a characterization of twinship that is echoed in at least
one strain of twin folklore and mythology. And although a clinical
understanding of twin psychopathology is germane to the current
task, the primary interest of the present work is to explain normal
twin development, with its attendant stresses.

The idea that twins encounter undue difficulties in identity formation is pervasive. In an interesting clinical paper, Joseph and Tabor
(1961) describe a twin in psychoanalysis who on one occasion, while
standing at a bus stop, happened to glance at a store window where he
caught his reflection. The patient was momentarily quite confused as
to whether it was he or his twin brother whom he saw reflected in the
window—a distortion that was perhaps accentuated by the regressive
process of his treatment. Observations like this are frequently reported to psychoanalysts and psychotherapists who have twins in
treatment. There is some support for the notion that identity conflicts
of this nature, though perhaps less acute, are not limited to twins who
have psychological problems but rather are a general characteristic of
twin psychology. Even studies of normal twins suggest this (e.g.,
Paluszny & Gibson, 1974). In one fascinating, detailed developmental study, Malmstrom (1978) presents a pair of normal identical twins
between the ages of twenty-five and forty-five months in which the
early emergence of complications in identity formation are evident.
These twins used a double name (both of their names combined as a
single name) for themselves. In addition, they used singular verbs in
reference to themselves together and often used the pronoun *me* as a
twin referent. At thirty-six months the twins were reported to have
had the idea that "it was possible for them to merge . . . they talked as
if they considered themselves one." Furthermore, some of their con-
versations were about dreams which they seemed to believe they could
share. For example, the fluidity of their self boundaries was high-
lighted by the following observation when the twins were forty-one
months: "One subject is afraid of the other's dreams." Reports from
mothers of twins suggest that these observations are common (see
chapter 7).

Our popular mythology about the difficulties that twins encounter in identity formation may contain a large kernel of truth; but most of our explanations are less than satisfactory. These explanations frequently emphasize the fact that twins "look alike" as the prime contributing factor in these developmental problems. Despite its obvious appeal, this is an extremely inadequate explanation on a number of grounds. For instance, it does not account for similar stresses in nonidentical (including opposite-sex) twins reported by Glenn (1966). Further, as already noted, in some instances even siblings who are close in age, though not twins, develop similar psychological characteristics.

The notion that physical similarities account for difficulties in identity formation is especially naive when it is viewed as an early and determining influence on the twin infant's development, since it fails to appreciate the perceptual and cognitive limitations of the human infant early in the first year of life. For example, Ackerman (1975) suggests that for each twin the other twin "is largely a mirror reflection of itself" hence leading to difficulties in identity formation. In addition to being limited to identical twins, this explanation assumes that from a very early age a twin (or any child for that matter) is able to recognize that the "other," that is, the twin sibling, "looks like me." The problem with the explanation is that for a child, knowing "me," in the sense of recognition which these explanations imply, is a highly complex and developmentally advanced capacity. Even for children who do not have difficulties with identity formation, it takes quite some time before they can recognize themselves as separate individuals. For example, mirror studies suggest that children are unable to recognize themselves in the mirror until they are about eighteen to twenty-four months of age (Amsterdam, 1968). Similar results have been found for self-recognition in photographs (Mahler et al., 1975). By age two, however, considerable evolution has taken place in identity development. Thus, the mirroring explanation for twin difficulties in identity formation points to two related questions: at what developmental juncture and through what mechanisms do these difficulties bear upon twin development?

To answer these questions it is necessary to begin with a description of the rudiments of the process of identity formation in infancy. In this manner, we will have available to us an outline of how children develop a sense of themselves as individuals. Clearly this developmental process is intricate and subtle and evolves over several years. In many respects, it continues throughout life (Erikson, 1968; Modell, 1968). However, by examining the early years when the necessary building blocks for identity formation are being placed, we will best be able to understand the indispensable ingredients of this process and how it affects twins.

Before proceeding to a description of this early period of psychological development, it is necessary to state how the term *identity* is being used here, since this is one of the most elusive and difficult of psychological concepts. Identity is derived from a great variety of developmental experiences. These range from feelings of a purely biological nature, which stem from bodily sensations as they relate to a basic core of being, to feelings about what sort of person one is in a more distinctly psychological sense. The relationship between one's sense of identity (and its cohesiveness and stability over time) and early development is quite complex. How aspects of experience evolve and are represented internally as psychological realities about "who are we" is crucial to our understanding of "identity confusion" and related psychological phenomena in twins. These psychological representations, whether they are actual mental images or vague and inarticulate feelings about oneself, are the core of identity. Identity, as used here, is composed of two experiential elements that are present intrapsychically in the form of self and object representations.[1] These representations have conscious, accessible elements and others that are unconscious but no less influential in how we experience ourselves.

Few self-representations come into being in isolation. Rather, a child's experience of itself is grounded in an interactive process with parents, other caregivers, and siblings. For example, a two-year-old may experience the wish to make messes as "bad." However, this self-representation is derived, in part, from an experiential history with an object (the child's mother, for example) who has attempted to communicate to the child that messes are not to be tolerated. Here we have a glimpse at another element in this child's psychological makeup—

---

[1] The term *object* is being used here in the traditional psychoanalytic sense. Thus, it does not refer to the inanimate world but rather the nonself world of people.

namely, in addition to a self-representation of being a "bad messy child," he also has an object-representation of mother as punitive or unaccepting of his wish to be "messy." The image might well be inaccurate, since it is derived from and subject to the limitations of a child's capacity to understand mother's adult motivations.

The process of developing these self- and object-representations is a unitary one since it is through the same interaction that both are created. The self-representation implies an object-representation, and vice versa. Thus, when speaking of identity formation as intimately connected to self- and object-representations, I am referring to one's experience of self and the world which is derived from these interactions. The history of our interactions with others is the medium through which we develop a sense of identity. This is even true of our physical experience to a greater degree than many would expect. For example, the infant develops a "body self" or "body ego" during the first six months of life as it develops the awareness that the body forms a single organism with definite physical boundaries (Jacobson, 1954). The early establishment of these body boundaries, however, is linked to being held by the mother as much as it is to the body exploration common of infants (Spitz, 1965). Thus, children whose parents express a degree of ambivalence and rejection through their physical interactions may develop distorted body images and a sense of themselves as defective, regardless of their actual physical characteristics. Accordingly, one would expect this view of the child to be communicated in a number of ways throughout the child's development. The primary interest here, however, is the interactive manner through which our sense of ourselves and of others develops.

Clinical experience teaches us that, as development proceeds, early self- and object-representations do not simply disappear. Rather, they influence subsequent experiences of ourselves and others. In addition to being detectable in a more derivative form in subsequent relationships, however, self- and object-representations also continue to be present in archaic forms which may emerge under stressful circumstances, in psychopathological disorders, or in the course of psychotherapy. We can think of identity as being composed of the evolution and reorganization of our object relations (which includes both self- and object-representations), as a distillate of this personal history, while simultaneously being something of a record of those experiences, in which earlier characteristics are not simply assimilated but may continue to exist in their archaic forms as well (Kernberg, 1966).

It would be clear that, as a function of a range of developmental experiences, our self- and object-representations are multifaceted. Thus, our illustrative child with a "messy" self-representation might easily have other self-representations of being "productive" or being "good" with corresponding object-representations of the praising, rewarding, or proud mother. Together these two psychological strands, the self- and object-representations, over time, reflect and encompass a wide range of complexity in psychological experience in the formation of identity. The quality and structure of these representations determine the degree of cohesiveness of the identity formed. However, in defining identity as composing one's internalized self- and object-representations, it should be understood that identity is a more comprehensive gestalt and is not reducible to a simple additive formula.

The psychological processes through which self- and object-representations become structured adequately requires, among other developmental achievements, the maturation of the child's cognitive capacities. Cognitive maturation enables these experiences to become structured intrapsychically through the mechanism of internalization (see Meissner, 1981). These representations are structured very gradually. Initially the child's self-representations are fragmented and limited, as are the representations of the object world. This is primarily because cognitive limitations and general lack of ego development characterize the human infant in the first months of life (Hartmann, 1958). There is an intimate relationship between the child's developing cognitive capacities and the developing sense of self and object, since the latter is based on the characteristics of a child's capacity to experience the world and himself in it. These developmental limitations, as well as the quality of the child's interactions with others in the environment, determine the character of early intrapsychic representations, which will only become fully integrated and structured over time.

It should be readily apparent that identity formation covers a broad range of possible developmental resolutions which may have varied implications for the quality of an individual's psychological functioning. By linking the question of identity formation to the development of object relations in general, and ego development in particular, a broader array of psychological functions becomes directly relevant to this discussion of psychological development (Nagera, 1981). Since the interest here is to formulate a more comprehensive understanding of the psychological development of twins, much of the subsequent discussion will not necessarily focus on the question of identity formation in isolation but will view this question as embedded in the broader developmental question of twinship. With key considerations now outlined, we take a more detailed look at the early psychological development of the child to see more clearly the special circumstances of twin development.

Two Developmental Stress Points:
Early Infancy and Separation-Individuation

The earliest contributions to psychological development begin in the first weeks of life in what is termed the "normal autistic phase" (Mahler et al., 1975). Although we know that infants are capable of relatively complex perceptual tasks at birth and that they are highly responsive to, and interactive with, external stimuli (Brazelton, Tronick, Adamson, Als, & Wise, 1975; Condon & Sander, 1974; Stern, 1974), the capacity to comprehend that these stimuli come from outside oneself is extremely restricted because of the infant's lack of cognitive maturation (Jacobson, 1954). Generally speaking, investment in the external world is limited in a strictly social sense. The infant awakens under the impact of internal states or other tension-producing conditions, only to drift back to sleep as homeostasis is regained. The infant's periods of wakefulness during the first two months are usually limited to those times during which this internal biological equilibrium is disturbed. Otherwise, the newborn spends much of its early life in a state akin to fetal life. Nevertheless, even during these first two months, the infant is able to respond to external stimuli and learns to recognize voice tones, characteristic ways of being held, and familiar scents, among other things. While these experiences are strongly reflexive in nature and are for the most part "wired in," and while they are not subject to cognitive representation as such (except in the sense described by Piaget, 1937, during the

sensorimotor period), these experiences play a significant role in lay-
ing the groundwork for personality development.

Of particular importance for our understanding of twin development are the developmental events that begin with the eclipse of the
normal autistic phase and the development of the symbiotic phase and
continue throughout the first year. These events can be examined from
a number of different theoretical vantage points, each of which varies
somewhat in emphasis as well as in the specific ages which they view
as most important. However, all focus on the first year of life and on
similar dimensions of the infant's interpersonal context. The *symbiotic*
period will be examined first as a way of conceptualizing the specific
developmental situation of twinship at this early juncture. Second,
a broader tradition of developmental theory will be drawn from,
specifically, the perspectives of *attachment* and *reciprocity*. These three
perspectives will be used to illustrate the first point of unusual stress
in twin development.

Symbiosis. By about two months of age, the infant gradually enters
into what Mahler (1963, 1968) terms the "normal symbiotic phase,"
so called because of the infant's pervasive dependence on the primary
maternal figure. This period includes the earliest and most rudimen-
tary awareness of mother as external. Although the normal symbiotic
phase is only several months in duration, ending by around six
months when the infant is able to begin to differentiate (Mahler et al.,
1975), it is a crucial phase. This is primarily because the infant has
begun to experience the mother as extremely important, and although she is not experienced as altogether separate from the self,
neither is she altogether fused with the self. A pervasive ambiguity
exists between self and other. For example, the infant may sense that
mother responds to needs because she is part of oneself, while the
infant simultaneously begins to sense that she is a separate person.
This progress in the infant's capacity to have a somewhat more realistic
assessment of self and object is facilitated by progressing cognitive
maturation. However, the primary psychological characteristic of the
normal symbiotic phase is the infant's relative incapacity to distinguish "I" from "not-I." For the infant, inside and outside are only
gradually becoming sensed as separate.

Mahler's work suggests that optimal development is fostered by a healthy symbiotic relationship between mother and infant in which the infant is able to experience himself or herself firmly within a symbiotic matrix with the mother. Here, the mother's empathic, sensitive contact with her infant creates a psychological environment in which the infant is neither frustrated nor engulfed excessively. In this context the infant is able to thrive, for such a nurturant environment permits the infant to develop the confident expectation of security, knowing that one's needs will be met.

For the infant to develop such a confident expectation within the symbiotic matrix, the mother must be what Winnicott (1960, 1962) terms "good enough," that is, a mother who is capable of adequately sensing and responding to her infant's needs. Some frustration, of course, is ongoing and inevitable in development. Although it is impossible to create a developmental context for an infant which is free from frustration, excessive frustration experiences can severely impair and even arrest an infant's subsequent psychological development. Winnicott's emphasis is on being good enough rather than on being perfect. It is this good-enough mothering that affords the child a psychologically nutritive "holding environment" during the normal symbiotic phase and beyond. If the relationship between mother and infant during the symbiotic phase is adequate, then the relationship with the mother "lights—the infant's—way to the small familiar world outside their commonly shared orbit" (Kaplan, 1978, p. 28). The first major developmental stress related to twinship is most likely at this very juncture, as the child moves through symbiosis prior to beginning the process of separation-individuation.

By the close of the normal symbiotic phase, most infants have developed a specific bond with their mother. They actively and selectively seek her. By five or six months, twins have clearly become aware of each other as well; they recognize and are affected by each other. Leonard (1961), for example, describes twins as having a soothing effect on one another at this age. Furthermore, as the capacity to imitate begins to develop, twins may take each other as imitative objects. Mothers of twins who are of this age will quickly attest to the fact that their twins are quite aware of each other and often seem to enjoy being in each other's company.

It is easy to inflate the nature of the twin relationship at this point. There are great limitations to each twin infant's capacity to respond to the other. The most important interactions for the twin infant, as is true for the nontwin infant, center on primary maternal figures. Feeding, bathing, changing, holding, and the sort of affectively synchronous play to be described shortly—these are the central experiences of the five- to six-month-old infant, and they place the mother firmly in the forefront of the infant's emerging consciousness of the world.

A number of circumstances change the usual mother-infant relationship for twins during symbiosis, potentially increasing the amount of stress experienced by a twin infant. For example, the reality of having to share the mother is likely to lead to increased frustration for twins from a very early age (Joseph, 1961). Logistically it simply takes a mother of twins longer to tend to the needs of her twin infants than to the needs of a single child. The empirical research supports this view. Gosher-Gottstein (1979) found that mothers of twins spent 35 to 37 percent of their time on infant-related activities, as opposed to 22 to 29 percent for mothers of singletons. On all infant-related tasks, mothers of twins had less time to spend on each child than did mothers of singletons. Similarly, Lytton (1980) concluded from his detailed observations of twin families that twins dramatically alter the climate of relations between children and their parents. He found that twinship affected both the quantity *and* quality of parent-child verbal exchanges. For example, twins required more overt parental verbal control than did singletons. Lytton also found that there was a trend for twin parents to be somewhat less responsive to their twins' distress and bids for attention. Lytton concluded: "The presence of two children of the same age in the home . . . [alters] the environmental contingencies to which children are exposed. In terms of the immediate harsh reality, it simply doubles the demands on mothers' and fathers' time, effort, and patience" (p. 79).

For these reasons, twinship often means that there is an increased amount of frustration for each twin infant than would ordinarily be the case. The empathic requirements of good-enough mothering are harder to achieve for the mother of twins. Furthermore, the reality of having to share mother may mean that each twin may never have spent sufficient time alone with the mother within the symbiotic orbit

(Coombs, 1978). These circumstances alter the nature of the relationship of each twin to the mother.

Supporting evidence for the notion that mothers of twins may find it difficult to be optimally responsive to their twin infants during this period is readily obtained. Both in interviews and in their questionnaire responses (see chapter 7), mothers of twins described the stressful nature of their twins' first year. For example, adjectives such as "draining" and "exhausting" were common in their descriptions. Furthermore, virtually all of these mothers made a special point of noting how important it is for a mother of twins to get adequate additional support during the twins' first year. If one juxtaposed the expectations for an adequate symbiotic phase with the actual circumstances governing this period for twins, such a contrast might be summarized as follows: at the developmental juncture when a mother is uniquely all important to the infant, the mother of twins is most likely to feel overwhelmed by the demanding task of meeting the needs of two infants at the same time.

As Mahler's work (1963, 1968, 1975) clearly indicates, if there is a problematic relationship with the mother during symbiosis, in which a securely based relationship has not been sufficiently established, the post-symbiotic stress of developing a sense of separateness will be more threatening to the child. In addition, the early potential for increased frustration may similarly leave the child with insufficient ego resources with which to effectively meet the developmental tasks ahead (Mahler, 1968). Thus, one sees here the potential disruption of the normal symbiotic phase for twins. The circumstance of twinship may significantly alter the usual conditions governing a child's passage through symbiosis in preparation for the separation-individuation process. A twin, for these reasons, may feel additionally threatened and vulnerable when faced with the growing awareness that infant and mother are separate people with different needs and that they are not magically linked within a common symbiotic orbit.

Attachment. A second and related vantage point on the developmental complications of twinship is attachment theory. Ainsworth's (1964, 1969; Ainsworth & Bell, 1974; Ainsworth, Blehar, Waters, & Wall, 1978) work on attachment—the affectional bond between an infant and its caregiver—centers on this same developmental period when, in Mahler's framework, the child first establishes an adequate symbiotic relationship with mother and then, slowly, using the symbiotic matrix as foundation, begins to emerge into a broader personal and social world.

Ainsworth (1967, 1972) suggests that there are three phases associated with attachment during the first year of life. The first is termed *preattachment*. However, this earliest form of attachment is somewhat indiscriminant, because the stimulus need not be a particular person, as in the infant's smiling response at two months (Spitz, 1965). This first phase of attachment is brought to a close with the enhancement of vision as an orienting mode for the infant, at around two or three months of age. Ainsworth calls the second phase *attachment in the making*. Here the infant's orientation and signals (what Bowlby, 1969, termed "attachment behaviors") are directed toward a discriminated figure or figures. This discrimination is evidenced primarily in the way in which the infant seeks to establish and maintain contact with different figures as well as in the ease with which these figures can comfort the infant in distress. Finally, Ainsworth suggests that at around six months, but usually somewhat later, the phase of *clear-cut attachment* is reached. The primary hallmark of this phase is found in the active use by the infant of a variety of behavioral systems, such as locomotion and vocalization, with the aim of attaining engagement with a clearly discriminated figure (usually mother).

In Ainsworth's view, the infant seeks to establish a degree of "affective synchrony" with the primary caregiver. However, the infant now discriminates who the person or persons are with whom he or she wishes to attain affective synchrony. The infant will not easily accept substitutes for these primary attachment figures at this age. Sroufe and Waters (1977), two key attachment theorists, emphasize that attachment must be thought of as the product of the interaction between caregiver and infant. Hence, this concept of affective synchrony is intimately related to Winnicott's good-enough mothering and the mother's empathic capacity to respond to her infant's varying states.

Ainsworth's and her colleagues (1978) distinguish three general patterns of attachment. This is important because the attachment classification of an infant (secure, avoidant, and ambivalent) is directly a function of the character and quality of the mother-infant relationship. Thus, alterations in developmental context have potential implications for the security of attachment, since these affect the mother-infant relationship. Attachment theorists have demonstrated that there is an important relationship between the quality and characteristics of the particular pattern of infant-mother attachment and infant's subsequent level of adaptation. For example, Matas, Arend, and Sroufe (1978) found that quality of attachment at eighteen months predicted toddler competence at two years: infants who were assessed as being securely attached at eighteen months of age were judged to be more competent (more enthusiastic, cooperative, and in general more effective) than insecurely attached infants in independent assessments. In a later study, Arend, Gove, and Sroufe (1979) found that individual differences in security of attachment at eighteen months were significantly related to teacher assessments of "ego resiliency" when the subjects were four to five years old. Securely attached infants were rated as more resilient. Further, children who as infants had secure attachment relationships scored higher on all three measures of curiosity that were employed in this study. These findings further support the notion that developmental contexts that impinge in a significant way on the establishment of a secure attachment may have long-term consequences for the child's general level of adaptation.

Although attachment theory has not been applied empirically to the study of twinship per se, a study conducted by Hock, Coady, and Cordero (1973, reported in Ainsworth et al., 1978) offers support for the thesis that twins may encounter unusual stress during the first year of life. Although this study was not specifically of twinship, their sample included fourteen twins and seventeen singletons. These authors found significant differences in mother-infant attachment between the two groups and hypothesized that these differences might be due to greater difficulty on the part of twin mothers in responding promptly to their infants' signals. In commenting on this hypothesis, Ainsworth et al. suggest that this explanation is congruent with their findings that differences in mother-infant attachment classifications are associated with behavioral differences among mothers.

The findings of Hock et al. must be regarded with some caution since theirs was not a study of twinship and since their sample is small. However, their findings are in keeping with the thesis being presented here—namely, twinship may alter the mother-infant relationship in important ways during the first year of life, and these altered developmental circumstances may have negative implications for the subsequent adaptation of some twins.

Reciprocity. Twin development during the first year can be examined from a third vantage—the concept of reciprocity. We know from a variety of sources that the human infant is born with an innate capacity for interactive behavior. Condon and Sander (1974), for example, have demonstrated the newborn infant's capacity to enter into "interactive synchrony" with the human voice, by which they mean that the body movement of infants tends to become synchronized to the rhythms of the adult voice, regardless of the language employed (including nonmaternal language). Similarly, the work of Brazelton, Koslowski, & Main (1974) suggests that social reciprocity is an innate potential, which the infant possesses at birth. His work indicates that infants experience human stimuli differently from inanimate stimuli, even at three weeks of age. And by six weeks, judges can reliably determine whether an infant is being presented with human versus inanimate stimuli by the infant's movement alone (Brazelton, 1974). Like Ainsworth, Brazelton argues that the infant has a goal orientation toward reciprocity, which he also terms affective synchrony. The infant attempts to establish, and then maintain, affective synchrony with the mother. Furthermore, he suggests that this interaction is a mutually regulated system in which both partners modify their actions in response to the feedback provided by the other. While the infant possesses an innate potential toward achieving a reciprocal relationship in which an affective synchrony is established, the other is required to bring this potential into fruition.

Brazelton's work is intimately related to the work of Spitz (1946, 1965), who has discussed the finely tuned, reciprocal, bidirectional interaction that develops between infant and mother in normal development. In this interaction the signals that are exchanged between the two participants are continually undergoing a transformation as each modifies behavioral responses to the other. Spitz's (1946) work with infants suffering from "hospitalism" documents the catastrophic consequences of environments where this dialogue is absent. Institutionalized infants he studied developed major lags in motor, language, and cognitive development and were significantly more prone to disease despite living in the most sanitary of conditions. While the latter is clearly an extreme circumstance, it is useful for underscoring the importance of reciprocity for healthy development. There is other evidence that the development of an effective bond between infant and caregiver, a bond that Brazelton et al. (1974), Spitz (1946, 1965), and others have argued is predicated on the establishment of an adequate level of reciprocity, is of great importance. For example, Brody (1956) has shown that there is a connection between smoothly successful, satisfying nursing experiences and the development of attention span and concentration, a finding which suggests that the establishment of adequate reciprocity (the feeding situation is the testing ground par excellence for reciprocity) has direct developmental implications.

Because of the newborn's overall level of immaturity, the infant requires relatively sensitive handling to protect it from excessive amounts of tension and distress, while also requiring appropriately modulated stimulation for optimal maturation to occur. According to Bibring, the mother's empathic interest in relating to the newborn is crucial to maintaining the bond between them (Bibring, 1959; Bibring, Dwyer, Huntington, & Valenstein, 1961). Reflecting the complexity of the processes that contribute to the establishment of reciprocity, Escalona (1963) has demonstrated that not only are individual variations in the child and in the mother important but so is the particular fit between the two.

Part of what is at stake in terms of establishing an adequate level of reciprocity centers on the capacity of the mother and infant to adapt to one another. For example, an oversensitive and excitable infant may be better off with a mother who is flexible and empathically soothing and consistent. On the other hand, an infant who is inactive and lacking spontaneity is best off with a mother whose empathic response leads her to stir her child's interest more actively. This type of mother provides the external stimuli that such an infant requires to bring it into active contact with the world around it (Escalona, 1963; Silverman, 1980). Interaction between the infant's innate disposition and the mother's characteristic modes of intervention leads to the emergence of basic patterns of perceiving and responding to the external world and to internal states (Silverman, 1980).

Twinship may pose a problem to this process. The essence of it can best be presented by again citing the work of Newman and his colleagues (1937): "One of the most striking facts that came to light in our studies of identical twins reared together is that the two members of a pair are never truly identical but differ more or less with regard to all their characteristics and that they differ sometimes to a disconcerting degree" (p. 36). Needless to say, this circumstance clearly holds true for nonidentical twins as well.

In a more recent work, Allen et al. (1976) have similarly found that while identical twins may be the same genetically, they nevertheless show significant constitutional differences. All of the variants of the reciprocity hypothesis share an emphasis—namely, that fine tuning, based on mutual accommodation and adequate empathic flexibility by the mother, is required to establish an adequate level of reciprocity in the mother-infant relationship. In this context the difficulty posed by twins becomes clear. The mother of twins is faced with the unusual difficulty of needing to synchronize herself to two infants simultaneously. This alone is a burdensome task. It becomes an even greater burden when each of the twin infants may have different qualities and characteristics to which the mother needs to adjust. This is particularly a problem when we take into account Escalona's (1963) suggestion that the mother's character structure and general psychological organization contribute significantly to the range of accommodations possible as well as to those she finds easier to make. It is possible, for example, that one twin's disposition, more than the other twin's, fits more easily with the mother's psychological characteristics. It may be relatively easy for the mother to be good enough, in Winnicott's terms, with one twin, while it may be considerably more difficult for her to be good enough with the other. The complication of having to attain an adequate affective synchrony with two infants who may be quite different must be added to the difficult reality of attempting to meet the needs of two infants at the same time, regardless of the ease of fit which the mother may have with either of them. For this reason, twins may experience increased stress during this period.

With minor variations, the symbiotic, attachment, and reciprocity perspectives all emphasize the importance of the first year of life in the development of the child. In particular, these theorists underscore the centrality of the mother-infant relationship in determining the child's subsequent psychological organization. These issues become vitally important to understanding twin development insofar as twinship constitutes an alteration of the developmental context.

One illustration from a mother of identical twins captures these issues poignantly. Her response to the question, "Describe what was most difficult for you as a mother when the twins were infants" was as follows:

From the very first couple of weeks on, B wanted to eat frequently—every two and one-half hours. I tried to stretch him out but couldn't because he gained very slowly the first two months, and the doctor said he needed every ounce. Because he cried to be fed, I also fed M, and B was never patient—a habit which was picked up by M and which became a problem as they grew older because they always *hollered* for their formula and then their food—I had always to have everything ready (warm, in bottles, or dish, etc.) just when they wanted it or their crying made me nervous it was so demanding and intense. At fifteen months they are only in their fourth week or so of being able to quietly (somewhat) wait while I prepare their meal (they are quiet *only* if they wait in *highchairs*).

That these differences reflected different developmental circumstances is best captured in this same mother's description of the process of feeding her twins during infancy: "[I] breast and bottle fed simultaneously for two weeks, then went to formula—B always hungered first, but I also woke up M when B cried. My husband and I wrote the day, time, and how much formula was consumed or water, each time. Because I fed them together, M tended to get too heavy, and I had to eventually limit him to six ounces at one feeding while letting small, thin B eat all he desired."

One can see from these vignettes not only that the first year might be exhausting but that the experiences of each twin might be quite different subjectively. M, for example, is initially fed whether he's hungry or not. Later, however, because this feeding schedule has made him overweight, since it is not in synchrony with his own digestive cycle, his food intake must be limited. Clearly, each infant already has a developmental context which is quite different. Furthermore, these differences in the twins translate to different psychological characteristics to which the mother must try to adjust. In this case, the mother chooses not to adjust to each infant because it would be too exhausting to do so. Instead, she attempts to make one infant conform to the other's natural feeding cycle. It is likely that this woman is more of a good-enough mother and provides a more optimal level of reciprocity for the infant whose natural biological clock is actually being responded to.

This dilemma is captured from a slightly different angle in the following example reported by McManus (personal communication, 1979). An expectant mother of twins who was interviewed prenatally hoped that her twins would be as similar as possible, since she felt that this would make it easier for her to minister to them. This wish persisted after the birth of her identical twins, although simultaneously this mother began seeing one of the twins as being very much like herself, while the other was seen as very much like her husband. This was, in part, an attempted resolution to the difficult logistics of parenting her twins, although it was also strongly influenced by the meaning of these children for the mother and father. As a result, one of the twins became "father's child," and was seen as being like him, while the other became "mother's child," and was seen as being like her. For this reason, each of these infants had a significantly different relationship with the mother. As with the first illustration, this accommodation reduced the emotional expenditure that the infants required of the mother. Since she was at home more than the father was, these differences changed the character of each twin's psychological environment. "Mother's twin" presumably had the benefit of a more optimal level of reciprocity, for the mother felt more connected with him than she did with "father's twin." This illustration is similar to the data presented by Lytton (1980, see chapters 1 and 2) in which he found that in a major subset of the twinships in his sample the twins had divided up the mother and father as objects of attachment. What this example adds, however, is the potential role of the parents' psychology in the formation of such differential attachments.

As twins negotiate this early developmental period, they are faced with issues that constitute the fundamental building blocks for subsequent development. Because of this, twins whose mothers have unusually limited psychological resources available to them are likely to be under greater stress; the same would be true for the single child. Similarly, twins whose psychological characteristics are unusually discrepant from their mother's may experience greater stress as well.

The Second Stress Point: Separation-Individuation

The second point of special stress in twin development occurs during what Mahler (1972) terms "rapprochement" when the toddler is around fifteen to twenty-four months of age. At this time the issues associated with one's developing sense of separateness and autonomy reach a peak. This is particularly true of the rapprochement crisis at around eighteen months. For every child, separation and autonomy are both a driving force and a source of anxiety and concern. The autonomous level of functioning may be highly sought after, indeed, insisted upon, yet the child is simultaneously sensitive that this autonomy implies giving up the gratification of a more dependent relationship to mother. Before going on to detail this key developmental period and its implications for twins, however, it is useful to fill in the developmental picture between symbiosis, which has just been examined, and rapprochement.

Thus far I have described the period during which the infant is just beginning to attain a sense of self and of the nonself world. In the symbiotic phase the child is still essentially undifferentiated—the sense that there is a world beyond oneself is limited. Mahler et al. (1975) have termed the separation-individuation process, which roughly spans the ages of six to thirty-six months, as the "psychological birth of the human infant," since it is during this period that the infant emerges in a definitive manner from a primarily organismic, reflexive mode of functioning into a fully psychological experiencing of oneself as a person in the world with an identity. Separation-individuation is generally divided into four subphases: differentiation (six to nine months), practicing (ten to fourteen months), rapprochement (fifteen to twenty-four months), and "on the way to" emotional object constancy (twenty-four months and beyond). Naturally, what is being described in separation-individuation is a developmental *process*. There is considerable overlap at the transition points between subphases; in addition, as is true of all developmental milestones, the ages are approximations which vary according to the particular characteristics of each child's developmental circumstances.

During separation-individuation the child grows from having an extremely limited awareness of himself and the outside world to experiencing himself as a separate, integrated person. Here the crucial steps toward identity structuralization, in the form of stable and richly diversified self- and object-representations, are taken. The separation-individuation formulation outlines the child's emerging sense of being a separate and autonomous individual, a development that is necessary in order to have a realistic sense of oneself and of the world in which one lives. In the realm of interpersonal relationships this means one who is able to form intimate relationships and yet not feel merged or dissolved into them. In terms of one's view of others, it means being able to experience them as separate, with their own characteristics and needs, as opposed to experiencing them primarily in terms of one's own need states. These two experiential modes— being able to form adequate intimate relationships and being able to experience others as separate from oneself—are the crucial developmental tasks for an individual, if one is to develop in an optimal, well-grounded, fully experiential manner.

The process of accomplishing this is obviously a psychological one. These characteristics are simultaneously made possible by, and reflected in, psychological developments. Ego development, and especially the development of cognitive capacities, makes it possible for a child to experience himself or herself and others in an increasingly differentiated manner. Simultaneously, circumstances in which the child is more often expected to act with greater autonomy (relatively speaking) also contribute to this process and become reflected in the child's psychology. Consequently, there are two contributing factors to separation-individuation—one strictly a maturational consideration, the other experiential. In reality these two processes cannot be effectively distinguished. They are fully interdependent, since part of what makes the child capable of comprehending his own separateness and autonomy is the emergent cognitive capacity to do so, while in turn this capacity is fueled by the nature of the child's experiences in the world.

The child's movement through the separation-individuation process is reflected intrapsychically in the development of increasingly separate self- and object-representations. Because of the interdependence of these processes, some children who have achieved sufficient cognitive maturation to effect a separation of self- and object-representations are unable to do so fully. This is because the characteristics of the relationship with the mother preclude the experiences which are necessary to attain such intrapsychic differentiation. For example, a mother may treat the child as if the child were not a separate person from herself. Such a mother might continually project upon the child her own motivations and needs, thereby treating the child as if he or she were a part of herself. Similarly, such a mother might feel threatened by her child's transition from being helpless and dependent to functioning on a more autonomous level because this relationship has been meeting her own dependent needs. Such a mother would attempt to forestall the process of separation-individuation. On the other hand, other mothers might bring their child's normal dependence on them to an abrupt and premature end, thereby not giving the child the opportunity to explore independence at his or her own pace.

Other factors complicating separation-individuation might include the birth of a sibling, which results in a significant change in the child's relationship with the mother. Similarly, losses due to divorce, the death of an important person in the child's life, or other major changes in the child's environment might also significantly complicate the child's movement through separation-individuation. Under any of these circumstances, a child might become rigidly preoccupied with the psychological issues of separation-individuation rather than be able to use these as the groundwork for further development.

It is important to emphasize that the separation-individuation process is to some extent a stressful developmental period for all children. While the amount of stress may vary depending on the specific nature of the child's environment, as well as on other developmental characteristics (such as the quality of the symbiotic phase, the level of language development, or other developmental milestones), ultimately what must be abandoned is the ubiquitous and comforting sense that mother and child are magically and powerfully connected. Perhaps the best indication of the amount of anxiety that the normal child experiences during this process is reflected in Winnicott's work on the transitional object (1962). It is no coincidence that children most often "invoke" the transitional object, that comforting, soft possession over which the child exerts complete control, precisely at the point in development when separation-individuation is getting under way. The transitional object is instituted just as the child begins to experience that the child and mother are separate. The transitional object facilitates this transition by allowing the child to maintain the illusion of merger with mother at stressful moments, especially those that may imply separation from her, such as bedtime (see Nagera, 1981). The prevalence of this phenomenon in children entering toddlerhood is testimony to how stressful the developmental tasks at hand really are.

As already noted, these issues begin to take form at the end of the normal symbiotic phase. This occurs when the young child begins to "hatch" psychologically (Mahler et al., 1975). The post-symbiotic period, during the first two subphases of separation-individuation proper (differentiation and practicing, respectively), is characterized by a rapidly increasing interest in the other-than-mother world. While mother herself is meticulously scrutinized and explored, the child increasingly investigates other aspects of the nonself world as well. This is greatly fueled by motor development. We characteristically see that infants who can crawl use mother as a home base from which to carry out these explorations. As the infant moves toward toddlerhood, actual contact with mother becomes less constant and overt. During the practicing subphase of separation-individuation, the toddler's apparent need for a mothering figure to hover seems to diminish and is supplanted by an active exploration of the environment. This exploration is characterized by a grand exuberance and sense of omnipotence which is only betrayed by occasional "emotional refueling," as the child periodically reestablishes contact with mother, or the "low-keyedness" which replaces the child's upbeat exploration when the mothering figure is actually inaccessible (Mahler et al., 1975).

During this important period in the twin relationship, the twins become increasingly involved with one another. This increased involvement is greatly enhanced by the fact that they are gradually able to interact with each other in more complex and gratifying ways. Their continuous presence makes them important players in the other-than-mother world with which they are increasingly engaged.

A major implication of this emergent intertwin relationship is that in some respects the ever-present twin comes to serve a comforting, soothing function, like the transitional object (Winnicott, 1953). The transitional object, a self-created substitute for the maternal environment, is also the recipient of a broad array of the young child's feelings, needs, and conflicts. In his discussion of relationships that serve a transitional function, Modell (1968) emphasizes the idea that differences between the self and the object are minimized, and the object is not acknowledged as being fully separate from the self (with implications for identity problems in twinship). To the extent that twins comfort and soothe one another, to the extent that each other's presence dilutes the anxieties inherent in early development (e.g., stranger anxiety or separation anxiety from mother), the transitional aspects of the relationship are enhanced. This characteristic of the relationship further serves to reinforce the twinship. While the extent to which one's twin serves this transitional function varies from twinship to twinship, and even within a particular twinship, it is likely that this transitional function is a common phenomenon in twinships, fostering mutual interidentification between the twins and serving to cement the twinship psychologically for each twin. In this manner twins become primary actors in each other's emotional lives.

The twin relationship differs from the child's tie to the transitional object in important respects. For example, unlike the transitional object, one's twin may not be as cooperative a recipient of one's projections as the transitional object is, especially as development proceeds. Further, unlike the inanimate transitional object, one does not outgrow one's twin. While there may be concerns within a family about how close the twins should be—Should they be in separate classes? Should they wear the same clothes?—the basic understanding in most families is that twins do and should have an enduring relationship with one another. Of course this is quite appropriate and what one expects of familial relations. However, in some circumstances this difference may actually serve to prolong or maintain the transitional function of the relationship, since the social forces that usually contribute to the relinquishment of the transitional object (such as a parent's sense that the child has outgrown a security blanket, or peer pressures that discourage the use of transitional objects) may not work the same way for twins. The environment may actually reinforce transitional aspects of the relationship in subtle ways.

Specific attention from others serves to accentuate the twin relationship. Although this is originally primarily a source of gratification for the mother of twins, it becomes increasingly a fact of life of which the twins themselves are cognizant, leading them to accentuate their relationship in certain ways. All of these factors contribute to the reinforcement of the twin relationship during the latter part of the first year and more so as development proceeds.

Rapprochement. The developmental forces that have become activated in the post-symbiotic period reach their peak during the rapprochement crisis, most commonly when the child is anywhere between eighteen and twenty-four months of age. This fact, coupled with the specific characteristics of twinship, make this an exceptionally difficult developmental period for twins. The rapprochement crisis is a developmental watershed in which the child comes face to face with the fact of separateness from primary figures, especially mother. Maturation of cognitive capacities, coupled with the relatively independent activities which have just been described during the differentiation and practicing periods, make the child aware that each of us is, in an irrevocable sense, separate from others. This means that parents, then, are not nearly as omnipotent as children want or need them to be, and that parents cannot magically know the child's thoughts and needs.

The emergent awareness of these psychological facts leads directly to the rapprochement crisis. This developmental crisis varies in intensity and duration as a function of the characteristics and quality of the child's care-taking environment, since these have everything to do with how easily the child is able to accommodate to this reality. The most common feature of the rapprochement crisis, and the phenomenon from which its name is derived, centers on the child's attempts to undo the sense of separateness from the mother, often by a transient return of clinging and other demanding behavior. The rapprochement child is characteristically ambivalent: on the one hand wishing to function autonomously, while on the other attempting to reconstitute the previous relationship with the mother, reflecting a reluctance to give her up. Thus there is an intense push-pull quality to the mother-child relationship. However, the degree of anxiety that the realization of separateness from mother brings is such that the less emotionally available the mother is during this period, the more insistently and even desperately the toddler will attempt to woo her back into an exclusive relationship (Mahler et al., 1975). From the perspective of separation-individuation theory, the crisis during rapprochement is considered *normal*. But as a developmental hurdle, it requires a suitable blend of available psychological resources and environmental supports, if it is to be surmounted without ill effects. As was true for the symbiotic phase, the circumstances of twinship can alter the developmental context of separation-individuation, making it unusually difficult for the twin to grapple with the developmental tasks at hand.

How twinship alters the developmental context of separation-individuation can be understood by looking more closely at the accentuation of the twin relationship during this period. As is true of all children of this age, the process of separation-individuation engenders a sense of anxiety that must be coped with. One readily available device for twins, as previously noted, is to use each other much like they would use a transitional object—that is, as ever-present, familiar soothers. Also, mothers emerging exhausted from the throes of their twins' first year of life find a welcome relief in the twins' developing capacity to entertain and comfort each other. In this way, a mother of twins may unwittingly foster a process in which the twin relationship can in some respects dilute her centrality and efficacy as a guide through separation-individuation.

Although the task of separation-individuation is the attainment of a sufficient measure of separateness and autonomy in psychological functioning, the mother's sensitive and empathic role in facilitating this process is as important here as it was during the normal symbiotic phase. The specific behavioral manifestations are different; the phase-specific issues are different; and the child's capacities are different. These differences alter what is required for good-enough parenting at eighteen to twenty-four months, but they do not change the need for a parent to be able to structure adequately the child's experience.

Mahler provides a model of what should transpire during separation-individuation between mother and child. To the extent that intertwin identification becomes accentuated during the course of development, a process somewhat parallel to that of the mother-child relationship should be at work in the twin relationship; however, there are obstacles to such a process. In the mother-child relationship, it is the mother who fosters (and in some instances enforces) the differentiation between herself and the child. But, at this early age, twins cannot bring this reality to bear on each other (even if they wished to). Parents may accentuate or dilute the extent of inter-identification between twins; yet even in instances where parents attempt to individualize their treatment of each twin, this may not always circumvent efforts by twins to use each other transitionally.

Two important observations serve to underscore the thesis that the rapprochement crisis is a very important developmental juncture for twins. First, during this period twins often begin to use the twinship defensively (for example, projecting feelings onto one's twin; Joseph, 1961). Second, increased deviation in language development is frequently reported for twins at this age (Lytton, Martin, & Eaves, 1977; Wilson, 1974). The problems associated with language development indicate possible difficulties during rapprochement, since this is the juncture during which language emerges as a functional process for the child. Twins tend to have less verbal interaction with their mothers than do single children (Lytton, 1980). This lessened interaction would make rapprochement more stressful for twins since the mother cannot regulate the child's experience as effectively. Twins, in turn, spend more time interacting with one another, which is often why twins develop a private language. This might be understood as a linguistic representation of the intertwin identification in which the private language reflects a special closeness that is not threatened by increasing differentiation. Since this private language can actually exclude the mother, it may also work defensively in some circumstances, maintaining within the twin relationship the sense of symbiosis which is threatened with her. This may be the reason why some mothers actually feel threatened by the twins' private language (Prall, personal communication, 1983).

These complications in the separation-individuation process, reaching a peak in the intensity of the rapprochement crisis, are common in twin development. Furthermore, as discussed earlier, twins may enter the separation-individuation process after having encountered a symbiotic phase which is unusually stressful as well. These two stressful junctures occur because twinship significantly alters the usual developmental context. Frequently the developmental experience of the twin is different in important respects from that of the single child, unless that child happens to have a sibling who is quite close in age. This altered experience gives the psychological organization of most twins certain common characteristics. In the following chapter three of these characteristics will be discussed: issues concerning self and object confusion, separation anxiety, and role complementarity. These issues will be related to difficulties in separation-individuation.

I emphasize again my observation at the onset of this chapter—namely, I have outlined here a set of developmental circumstances that give twin development a particular cast. I am not contending that this rendering does justice to all the possible variants of twin development; however, it may be a somewhat prototypical developmental pattern for twins. Further, these are the crucial issues in twin development. They suggest that the kind of twin one is (identical, fraternal same-sex, fraternal opposite-sex) may be less important than the specific manner in which these developmental hurdles are met by any given set of twins. This is the reason, for example, why some opposite-sex twins can be psychologically taxed by their twinship (Glenn, 1966; Orr, 1941), while some identical twins can emerge from this process without detrimental psychological effects.

More important, these developmental circumstances create a set of experiences that constitute an adaptational context. The presence of separation-individuation issues in twin personality organization are a testament to this adaptive process. Like the egos of some singletons, the egos of some twins can be overwhelmed by these early developmental stresses, resulting in personality organizations which are problematic and distinctly maladaptive. The question of the presence of separation-individuation issues in twin personality organization as a result of adaptation is distinct from the question of psychopathology. There is evidence, for example, that twins are underrepresented in psychiatric populations (Ainslie & Nagera, 1980; Paluszny & Abelson, 1975). It is most important that this distinction between adaptation and symptomatic compromise be kept in mind in the following chapters.

4

Psychological Issues of Twinship

This chapter will illustrate some of the psychological characteristics of twins that are either implicated by twin research or theoretically supported by the conceptualizations previously presented.

The clearest support for the developmental scenario described in chapter 3 is material suggesting that in various ways the consolidation of a cohesive sense of identity is made more difficult by the context of twinship. Such a consolidation is intimately connected with the elaboration of adequately demarcated psychological boundaries between oneself and others or through an adequate intrapsychic differentiation between self- and object-representations. Therefore, this is the arena in which it would be most useful to look for documentation of the thesis that identity consolidation is a point of vulnerability for twins.

A brief glance at the empirical literature makes it apparent that a good, operationalized definition of *identity* does not exist. The reasons for this are readily appreciable, for the concept of identity is extremely complex and impossible to confine to a given trait, behavior, or disposition. On the contrary, while it is an idea that can be grasped intuitively, the construct of identity is extremely elusive and fluid at any given point in development, not to mention across the life span. To illustrate these issues in the lives of twins, it is necessary to be descriptive, employing what twins have to say about themselves and their experience. Hard-core experimentalists will no doubt find such an approach rather unsavory. Nevertheless, knowledge, to be of value, must have some correspondence with what goes on in people's lives at a more immediate level. The issues which are posited to be at play in twinship will be described at this level.

Insufficiently differentiated self- and object-representations, or a tenuous consolidation of a sense of identity, might be illustrated in various ways. The clearest illustrations would seem to center on an overt feeling that one's sense of self can be lost, at least temporarily, that one's sense of self is seriously threatened in certain situations, or that the stability of one's sense of self is contingent upon another. Problems in identity consolidation do not manifest themselves only in this overt form. Other kinds of behavior, or other feeling states, also lend themselves readily to such a conceptualization, although here one might not necessarily be able to rely on the subject's own *sense* that the level of his or her identity integration is tenuous. For example, excessive dependence reflects a difficulty in independent functioning which is readily understandable in terms of the presence or absence of cohesiveness in identity formation. Experiencing oneself as part of a unit, in the absence of which one feels incomplete or only like part of a person, would be another example of a feeling state that is directly comprehensible in terms of the quality of identity formation. Finally, the rigid structuring of roles, often seemingly linked to sex-role stereotypes as seen in chapter 2, can also be understood as a kind of distortion of the identity formation process, insofar as the pool of possibilities of who one can be is somewhat rigidly and arbitrarily demarcated. Examples like this will be presented in this chapter to illustrate difficulties in identity consolidation.

It is important to bear in mind that twinship merely accentuates particular issues in development. As an adaptational context, it is not accurate to say that twinship predisposes one to certain psychopathological outcomes. The present thesis is that twinship, as a developmental situation, lends itself to characteristic patterns of functioning or characteristic issues. Every famiy constitutes a particular developmental context for the child. This context is a function of the psychological factors at work within that family which impinge upon the child. Developmentally, twinship is not in and of itself psychopathological; what determines that, as in any developmental situation, is the interplay between the child, including constitutional elements, and primary players in the child's environment. How this evolves into a set of concrete experiences, of day-to-day interactions, determines the extent to which a child's optimal development becomes enhanced or compromised. In the following descriptions, difficulties in identity consolidation are best thought of as points of vulnerability, which may be activated from time to time in the lives of these twins. *Every* individual has such vulnerabilities. Although these may compromise his or her optimal level of functioning in a given situation, they do not constitute a clinical syndrome.

Material in which twins give direct expression to the feeling that one's sense of self is tenuously organized will be presented first, through Darla's examples. She and her sister, Marla, MZ twins in their early thirties, lived in different cities but had frequent contact by phone and managed to visit each other once or twice a year. Darla indicated a tenuous sense of herself in situations that involved Marla as well as in nontwin relationships, such as those with her ex-husband and her parents. For example, Darla was divorced, and many of the characteristics of her marriage reflected a kind of personal subjugation to her husband that she experienced as depleting her identity. She had devoted herself to him entirely, putting him through graduate school. Darla's husband had abruptly left her immediately after finishing his studies, something that came as a devastating surprise to her.

Darla described how important this relationship had been for her: "I felt like I would have done anything for things to work out between [ex-husband] and I. It was real important to me—after putting a lot of time and a lot of money—two years of real hard-earned money. I'd put him through school. . . . It was a real hard summer when he left. . . . It dawned on me that I had given up my life to someone who as it turned out didn't want to put any energy into maintaining a really good relationship."

Later in this same interview Darla discussed one major source of tension in her marriage—namely, she didn't want to have children. The theme of giving up her self is quite strong:

"The things that he wanted from me I didn't want to give. I didn't want to have kids, and I didn't want to give up my whole life for everything that [ex-husband] wanted, and that's what I was doing. So that was a sad realization, but I feel like a stronger person for doing what I did and not going back to [where ex-husband lives], not giving up my self, which I didn't do. I don't know what I could have done [to get back together with him] without giving up part of my self."

Interviewer: "That was a possibility?"

Darla: "I don't know what would have happened, how I might have saved things, but I don't know what would have happened to *me* had I done that. It's sort of like giving up my self, which I had done a lot before."

Darla's identity was at stake in her marriage: her capacity to be a person separate from her husband and to keep her own best interests in mind was potentially compromised. These concerns were present in the context of her family as well.

"When I go home, sometimes I feel the need to show my family the things that I have back here [in city where she lives], or that my life is good and that I'm happy. School is difficult, but it's what I want. But you don't have any of those things, like for some reason I take a great deal of pride in having a place to live where I really feel good, and I can do what I want. This place [her apartment] is obviously no showcase, but for me it's sort of special, for some reason. So to pack a suitcase and just go away . . . I guess I just feel stripped of all this security when I go out there. One reason I didn't move out there—I was talking about my divorce, and mom said, 'Why didn't you come out here?' I just feel like that's not right. I don't want to just go out there and immerse myself in their life. I just want a life of my own, and it's going to take a while."

While it is apparent that these concerns about losing her sense of self are present in a number of important life contexts, to Darla they appear most strongly in the twin relationship. For example, Darla discussed why the twins don't live in the same city:

"I wouldn't want to live in the same city with Marla because we care about one another a lot. But *I want to have my own life* and I didn't—I think that twins can sort of psychologically feed off of one another. I think that can be true, and I didn't want to do that."

Interviewer: "What would constitute that in your relationship?"

"I think that Marla and I, feeling like we do about one another, if we were in the same city, well, first of all that would be impossible because we would drive each other *nuts*. We really can't be together, but living together all the time I think so restricts your life that the rest of your life space and things you want to do would be really confining."

Interviewer: "Is there a sense that you would end up too wrapped up?"

"Well, not like anything that we were going to merge into one person or anything like that [laughs], but just sort of like neither one of us could have a real individual life, that's very important to me—to have an individual life and an identity of my own. That's been a real important thing for me."

In another interview Darla observed:

"Being an identical twin oversensitizes you to the need for a unique and individual identity. In terms of my own achievements, my sister has always been a measuring stick, and this has always been unfortunate. One can't feel pleased about one's accomplishments if in being very successful that belittles the accomplishments of another person. It's unnecessary and destructive; it denies their individual potentials and encourages external evaluation that can have *disastrous* consequences. My sister and I have survived this continuous comparison rather well; however, the physical separation and healthy distance between us has allowed us to create our own individuality."

Darla's individuality appears to have required considerable effort. She must struggle to maintain it or to enforce it through such means as deciding where to live as a way of safeguarding that identity. Although it is likely that everyone must at times take steps to preserve a sense of identity, most people do not require this sort of effort. Darla makes it clear that this is a necessity for her when discussing what it is like to be in Marla's city for any length of time: "When I go out there, it could be that I feel somewhat ill at ease because I don't have *my* home, *my* friends, and so I'm going, fitting into Marla's life for a while."

In another interview Darla made this point more explicitly: "I feel like we could never live together mainly because I don't know if we just don't get along and our personalities conflict or more that we're just so much alike that it's really difficult for me to be around Marla for more than a week. I consider that a fairly long time, and I start feeling we have to do things separately. I think we're just so much alike that it is like losing a sense of self into this other person, and so you just have to sort of back up, because this person is—well we're just so much alike in so many ways. So that's one reason why we don't stay together and don't live in the same city."

Later in this same interview Darla noted that when visiting Marla:

"I never thought I was just moving into Marla's world and losing my own. I don't think that's true, but more like just losing a sense of identity. Maybe that's the same thing."

Interviewer: "What do you mean?"

"It's [identity], more something that's within me. It's not what I have, but I think maybe, too, things I have make me feel more secure about myself . . . maybe it's important to me to have space of my own. Marla and I are very much alike, and what makes us different is our surroundings, things that we have. The things that she has are a lot different from the things that I have. Maybe that's one of the things that makes us different. And when I go out there, I don't have those things, and then I just have *me*. When she goes into [city where their parents live], then it's just *her*, and we're very much alike then."

Darla provides us with a very clear and strong picture of a twin who is actively struggling to maintain a sense of her identity. This struggle is not limited to the twinship but also was evident in her marriage and in her relationship to her family. These concerns, however, appeared most acutely in her relationship with Marla. It is unlikely that these difficulties in identity consolidation can be explained exclusively in terms of twinship itself. For example, Darla and Marla's family of origin was chaotic and conflict-laden. Yet the twin situation and its related stresses probably contributed substantially to the fact that Darla is encountering psychological problems, particularly in the area of identity consolidation.

This was not the only twinship in which these concerns were evident. Debbie and Dianne, fraternal twins in their early twenties, were markedly dissimilar in appearance. Debbie was petite, small-boned, and attractive. Dianne, on the other hand, was overweight, broad-shouldered, and somewhat unattractive. During their joint interview Debbie remarked, "Because we don't look alike, no one even knew we were sisters unless we told them." This twinship is a good illustration of the fact that zygosity is not such a major factor in the determination of the psychological factors affecting twins.

Debbie and Dianne manifested a number of concerns regarding the stability and cohesion of their identities. For example, in the joint interview the twins described how different they were from one another and how their differences, rather than their similarities, were emphasized at home. In this context Debbie stated, "I felt like half a person as it was, so why try to be more like Dianne? I could never become a whole person."

Debbie voiced similar feelings about the cohesiveness of her identity. As with Dianne, this also came up as she discussed the importance of support. In Debbie's case, however, she was speaking directly about her relationship with Dianne: "A lot of times I'd call her for support, and I knew she would always be there, and she would get excited for me. . . . There was that bond there that she would really understand what I was feeling almost as if she was a part of me."

Like Darla, Debbie and Dianne express similar feelings about the tenuousness of their sense of identity; they describe feeling that their identity is intimately connected with, or is a function of, their twin.

Dependency

Although somewhat more inferential than direct statements about potential identity loss, distortions in dependency are readily understandable in terms of difficulties in self-object differentiation, since conflicts in this arena imply a degree of anxiety associated with functioning as an autonomous individual. These concerns might be reflected directly, as the twins discuss issues relating to dependency, although they might also be reflected in such issues as considerable anxiety around separation from their twin. In some instances, of course, these feelings might have become generalized to other people as well.

Debbie and Dianne provide a number of examples of this kind of interdependence. For example, in chapter 3 the use of one's twin as a comforter or transitional object was discussed. This was the case in this twinship. Both twins appeared to comfort one another, although Debbie served that function more often for Dianne. The following interaction between Debbie and Dianne illustrates this:

Dianne: "Although we fought a whole lot, we had this real deep interdependency."

Debbie: "Yes, the first day of kindergarten. Do you want to talk about that?"

Dianne: "Yes, I was the only kid in the whole place who couldn't cry."

Debbie: "I hated Dianne . . . but I felt a real strong bond between us. In kindergarten, I was real scared the first day, and I was crying too, but I was very comforted that Dianne was there, and that was a big deal."

Dianne: "We were shy about new situations, and it was just very comforting to have the other one."

Debbie: "Like going to birthday parties. We were very comforted by having each other there."

Dianne: "I think the most important thing to me in terms of dependency was Debbie's presence in social situations, just for her to be there; and especially when we were kids, she was much more easily likable with other people, and I was kind of shy, so that kind of took the pressure off of me, that I didn't have to stand alone."

It was especially evident in Dianne's interviews that dependency was still an area of concern in the present. Perhaps because her relationship with Debbie had been characterized by such ambivalence (as she says, they fought a great deal, yet they were tremendously interdependent), Dianne was presently apprehensive about intimate relationships and the issues of dependency that they inherently involve. In the context of describing these concerns Dianne noted, "When I have intense relationships with people, it kind of reminds me of my twinship relationship."

Interviewer: "Can you tell me about it?"

Dianne: "I think I feel kind of defensive, that I might be regressing or something. Sort of like an irrational feeling of mine that to become dependent with somebody else—because I'm always changing. But that could be because I think my feelings about my interdependency with Debbie was [that] we escaped together from what happened with our family, and sometimes I want to do that in life, and I'm afraid I'm going to do that with a person I'm having a relationship with. . . . Dependency scares me a lot because I think that, or at least it's been my experience in the past, that dependency with members of my family have really turned into horrible, ugly things and limited options a lot. . . . I think that whenever there is a dependency there is always a threat of it being taken away, and being dependent is being real vulnerable."

Later in this interview Dianne said: "It's hard for me to remember that I can be in control of situations even if I'm feeling dependent. I don't have to lose myself—I can still have choices."

Later Dianne added: "If I'm dependent, then I'm going to lose myself and things can get really bad." These feelings were scary for her: "It was like that relationship was so important to me and that support was so important to me, I didn't feel like I had personal strength."

The latter remarks make it clear that the link between dependency concerns and identity consolidation is a close and theoretically sound one.

In Debbie's individual interviews she reflected similar concerns. For example she described her negativity toward Dianne and the fact that as children she had often attempted to undermine Dianne's relationships with friends. She felt that these efforts were related to a fear of loss: "I was always very afraid of [Dianne's] getting another close girl friend because then I would feel like she was going to forget about me; so I would do all these vicious things trying to steal her friends away."

At a later point in the same interview, Debbie commented on these vicious things that she had done to Dianne, concerned that Dianne might never forgive her for those things done in childhood: "She means a lot to me, and if she never forgives me, that would be the worst."

Interviewer: "What do you mean?"

"That would be about the worst thing that could happen to me. If [boyfriend] left me, that would be bad, but I really love Dianne a lot, I feel a very strong bond to her, and if I feel that she never forgave me, that would be one of the worst things that could probably happen to me. . . . I would just feel deserted. As if a part of me would never really come back."

Debbie's interviews indicate a strong interdependence with her twin and considerable concern in the face of a loss or diminution of that bond. As with Dianne, Debbie's interviews also reflect the close association between the issues of dependence and identity consolidation (a breakdown of the twin bond would make her feel as if she were losing a part of herself).

It is evident from these fraternal-twin interviews that concerns about identity integration are not limited to identical twins. Opposite-sex fraternal twins, which one would expect to be the least likely to develop such concerns (since they do not look alike, and differences in gender naturally facilitate differentiation), also reflect these issues. For example, Martha and her twin brother, John, almost thirty years old, were close as children and had shared a bedroom until the age of eight. In describing their relationship, Martha noted, "We never argued like other siblings."

Martha and John were in the same classroom until the third grade, at which point they were placed in separate classes because their mother felt that "it was time that we be separated." Martha describes this experience:

"It was an extremely traumatic time for both of us. I don't remember it distinctly, but my mother said that I came home every day from school and cried, every day. I *do* remember crying a lot and being miserable and missing him a *great* deal. He missed me too; he would say he wanted to be with me. So in fact after that, in fifth and sixth grade, we were placed back in the same class again."

The twins' relationship was so close that Martha's marriage appears to have had a great impact on John.

Martha: "When I got married my relationship with my brother as I had known it came to an abrupt halt."

Interviewer: "Why was that?"

Martha: "He was probably resentful that I had found someone else, someone that I loved and was willing to move a long distance to be with [goes on to describe tensions in the relationship between John and Martha's husband]. To this day I don't like being around both [of them] at the same time because they are reduced to being like three-year-olds vying for my attention and affection. It makes me nervous. My husband has come to accept the fact that he can never understand our twin relationship. He couldn't understand the difference between being a twin and being a brother and a sister. . . . My husband feels like he has to please my twin, that he has to make amends for taking me away."

When John got married, Martha's feelings were not unlike his:

Martha: "Now my brother is married, and I can understand how he feels."

Interviewer: "How do you feel?"

Martha: "Very ambivalent. It was very, *very* difficult for me to see him with his wife-to-be before the wedding. I felt like she had all of his attention, completely, all of it. He was totally wrapped up in her and that hurt. It was really *really* painful, and I felt left out."

As with the previous subjects, the mutual interdependence between Martha and John is linked to considerable anxiety at the thought of possibly losing each other. For example, Martha described a recent dream:

"I remember this dream, and it was that John's life was somehow in jeopardy. I woke up and was totally convinced that this might be true. I was in a total state of panic. My first impulse was to call him and see that he was OK. I got out of bed and walked around the house and woke myself up fully, and I realized that it was a dream."

While dream interpretation requires caution and deliberation, even when one knows the dreamer well and has the benefit of the dreamer's thoughts about the dream itself, at a manifest level Martha's dream appears to reflect considerable anxiety at the thought of losing her twin brother.

The conceptualizations covered in chapter 3 suggest that one manifestation of the instability of self- and object-representations, and therefore identity, is separation anxiety. Both attachment theory and psychoanalytic theory, for example, rely heavily on the notion of separation anxiety as a developmental construct. Dependence is also intimately related to separation anxiety since anxiety of being separated from one's twin would presumably encourage the maintenance of greater interdependence.

Some of the subjects who participated in this study gave interesting examples of distress at separation from their twin. Cindy provides one such example in the context of discussing the difficulties associated with taking a trip:

"[I] like to travel, but there is always something in me that thinks about home a lot. Maybe it's a fear that something is going to happen to me, or to my family, and that if I am not in touch with them I couldn't know anything. Then I feel like, 'Well, if someone were with me . . . then that would be a little better, if something did happen or something happened to me.'"

Lindy, Cindy's twin, presented similar concerns about traveling by herself. When asked at one juncture during her interviews if these concerns might be related to being a twin, Lindy responded, "Well, yes, because mainly the person I would be thinking of going with [in order not to go by herself] would be Cindy."

A major event which both Cindy and Lindy discussed in their separate interviews was a trip taken by Cindy in high school. This is Lindy's depiction of that trip:

Lindy: "It was in eleventh grade, and it was the first time that we were ever separated."

Interviewer: "What was that like?"

Lindy: "She called me every night. She was there for—I don't remember how long she stayed, but I remember I was taking drivers ed. That Saturday I didn't know that she'd be there, and I remember coming in and seeing her, and I didn't want to get all emotional about it, but I was really glad to see her there!"

Interviewer: "How long was she gone?"

Lindy: "About a week—no, more than that, but it was the first time where we'd ever been at two different ends, where we couldn't see each other. It was different than, say, spending the night at an aunt's or something. For her to go away on a plane—that's what really *hurt* me—I mean, seeing her, I just had the feeling that she wasn't coming back. I said, 'What if she gets over there and she likes it?' All these different things ran through my head . . . I *cried* when the plane took off. I didn't cry when she was there, but I *cried* when the plane took off."

In his interviews, Tim also indicated a passing feeling that this kind of separation might lead to a more permanent loss. He described his concern regarding vacations and trips as follows: "I suppose when you are close to someone you always think that maybe if they go away on a trip or something that they may not come back."

Kathy and Christie are fraternal twins in their early thirties. Christie emphasizes that their closeness was an early pattern: "My sister and I were very close and always considered each other to be our best friends. [Describes the difficulties of starting new classes in school—prior to fourth grade.] We tended to cling to each other for support."

However, in college, Christie's dependence on the twinship created major difficulties for her as Kathy grew closer to her boyfriend. Although ostensible roommates, Kathy spent a great deal of time with her boyfriend. Christie was hurt and felt left out: "[Kathy] was supposed to care for my well-being, [but] I felt that I was lost. Like a fifth wheel."

Christie did not have a boyfriend at the time. However, shortly thereafter she met a man and married him somewhat precipitately. It turned out to be a poor marriage and ended in divorce a few years later. Christie feels that her dependence on Kathy is partially responsible for her poor selection of a marriage partner:

"I think it [the tensions between Christie and Kathy] had a lot to do with the fact that I got married as early as I did, because, as I said, it's very frustrating not to be able to resolve that major a conflict in your life. I met [ex-husband], and we started going out and seeing a lot of each other. I'm not trying to blame all my problems on her, but I think I leaned on him and developed that relationship more quickly than I might have if I'd had other plans and other people close that I could rely on for companionship. . . . When you've only known someone for a month, you don't tell them your deepest darkest secrets like you do your sister, *if* she's there to talk to. But she wasn't there to talk to. So, in retrospect . . . I really feel I relied on [ex-husband] a lot more quickly and became not dependent but intimate with him a lot more quickly, because of looking for something or someone whom I could be close to. I think that relationship developed—I don't think it would have developed at all if I hadn't been in that situation [with Kathy], but I just relied on him more quickly than I would have otherwise."

Cindy and Lindy described a more dramatic and acute anxiety about separation in going to college. The twins had planned to share a dormitory room, but because of a clerical error, they were assigned to different floors within the same dormitory. Cindy's reactions to this were quite marked:

"We tried to get a room together, and it got mixed up or something, and they didn't put us in together. I was really upset. When the papers came from housing saying where we were assigned to live, we found out we were in the same dorm but different floors, and I started crying. And Lindy said, 'Don't cry, what are you crying for? We can always get together.' But I said that it might not be that easy—I didn't see it that way—I was afraid of it, it was the first time we would be separated."

In another interview Cindy described the effects of the separation on her: "We were separated [in college], and—I didn't know where she was, and she didn't know where I was most of the time. And it was at times when I really wanted to talk to her and I just couldn't find her anywhere that I would really get upset, 'Where is she!'"

Interviewer: "What would you do? Would you look for her?"

Cindy: "Oh, yes! I would look and look, and sometimes I would ask so-and-so, and then I would go there and couldn't find her. I would get angry because I couldn't find her. I guess the same thing happened when she couldn't find me too, but there were really a lot of times I wanted to find her and couldn't. I would just be angry: 'Somebody should know where she is!' 'Somebody should try to help me!' It was anger at not being able to find her, and maybe a little at her for not being there, [but] really for not being able to find her."

A strong interidentification between twins can be thought of as related to high levels of dependency, although the manifestations might be considerably different. Both can be understood as reflecting an inner sense of oneself as inextricably connected to one's twin. Strong empathic reactions for one's twin—reactions in which the twin sibling's experience is also experienced as one's own—would be examples of such interidentification. Interidentification in this sense is related to a blurring of self- and object-representations insofar as self-object differentiation is temporarily lost.

A number of twin subjects, both MZ and DZ, reported incidents in which they had strong empathic reactions to their twin. The following example from Tim's interview is typical:

"There were times when, if Tom were punished for something, I'd feel so bad because he was being punished, or feel he was being hurt, because my Dad spanked him or something, then I'd get tears in my eyes—kind of sympathetic, I guess. I can remember Dad scolding us for fighting or something, or one of us was getting spanked for doing something. It happened to both of us. I remember Tom crying when I was getting hurt—or punished."

Similarly, Sandie described getting sick as children: "All through our childhood mother would get annoyed if one of us threw up. No sooner did she clean it up than the other did the same . . . without fail that always happened."

Interviewer: "Can you give me an example?"

Sandie: "One night Jean woke up and got sick, I hadn't felt sick, [but] seeing mother rush in, I just got sick too. Same with her [Jean] too, we used to think that it was the sight of vomit, but, if someone else gets sick, *it's less of a self-sickening thing*" (my emphasis).

Other examples suggest a greater pervasiveness of the sort of inter-identification seen here. For example, Cindy reported:

"I was just thinking about different times that I had defended [Lindy]. It hurt me as if the person was saying it about me, and really they were talking about her, but it just seemed like it was coming to *me* personally. Someone might say something to insult her, and I would say, 'Don't talk about my sister like that, that's my sister.' I would always defend her. I didn't want anyone to say anything bad about her."

This reminded Cindy of a specific example: "Some people say that they can tell the difference between us, because she is a little heavier now, because she's gained weight. So someone would say to me, 'I can tell you and your sister apart because she is fat and you are not.' Instantly, I said, 'She's not fat, there is a weight difference, but she's not fat.' It seems as though they were saying that I am fat."

In a similar example, Melissa discussed her reactions to a friend's complaint about Stephanie: "They'll tell me things that they don't like about Stephanie, [her reaction is], 'Well, don't tell me, because it's like a slap in *my* face! Go tell her!'"

The interidentification between these twins is clear. In these examples, they do not appear to be simply standing up for their twin. Rather, complaints about the twin sibling are also experienced quite personally, as if the complaints were about them.

Self as Part of a Unit

The difficulties in differentiating self and twin are evident in other material as well. For example, in numerous interviews the twins had ways of describing themselves and their experience which suggested the sense of themselves as members of a common entity. Some of these references were innocuous. For example, in discussing his salary with the interviewer, Tom stated, "Between us we make $20,000." In another interview, Tim said that when they were growing up he had often daydreamed that he and Tom were actually Siamese twins who had been separated. In one of her individual interviews, Lindy was discussing their birth. In this context she noted, "Both of us were under four pounds—three-and-a-quarter pounds—we barely made it because together we were almost seven pounds." Married couples may talk about their income as a joint figure, siblings usually do not. Similarly, it is unusual for one to hear an individual discuss his or her birth weight in terms of a composite figure. Sandie and Jean's Halloween memories, from chapter 2, in which they went to successive parties dressed as a two-headed monster or toothbrush and toothpaste have a similar ring to the examples we have just seen. These descriptions, as related to the question of identity formation, imply a sense of being incomplete, parts of a whole, or within a common boundary in which one's existence is inexorably linked to the other.

Tom presented a rather striking example of this sense of being part of a unit during his final individual interview, as he wondered about how what he said had fit in with what Tim had said during his interviews:

Tom: "I think that we answered questions pretty much the same— that's fine that we may think alike, but it also shows that we're dependent, that we're still dependent on each other, *like two ideas into one-type thing*" (my emphasis).

Interviewer: "Two ideas into one?"

Tom: "Yes, if you ask us something, we put our ideas together into one, rather than each of us coming up with our own answers. We've always done that—it's like a joke in our family."

In describing coming to college, Toni noted that the initial transition might have been somewhat difficult: "At first [coming to college] was kind of scary, but not as scary as it could have been because we were both together. It was really neat. We just experienced about everything together, and it was really nice. Whereas, *to be just one person*, it really is kind of scary" (my emphasis).

In this example Toni reflects the link between interdependence and the feeling that one is part of a unit. Here the loss of boundaries between Toni and Tracy is experienced as a kind of comfort; somehow it dilutes the anxiety and stress which might otherwise be part of a major life change such as going away to college. In fact this description is quite reminiscent of earlier examples of the comforting function of the twinship. Experiencing oneself as part of a unit also has its drawbacks. For instance, Toni, in describing the twins' popularity in high school, noted: "We were known as the '[last name] twins.' Sometimes I thought, 'Would I be as popular if there was only me?' I just didn't know. I couldn't answer that myself."

The close interidentification that can result in the feeling that one is part of a unit can also, through that very mechanism, interfere with a sense of perspective regarding oneself and one's accomplishments, talents, interests, and so on. Such a perspective is the hallmark of a firmly consolidated sense of identity. Through these illustrations Toni in effect highlights the double-edged nature of such intense interidentifications. On the one hand, the dependency engendered can be a great source of support and nurturance, especially in anxiety-provoking situations. On the other, that very interdependence can constitute an obstacle to an adequate demarcation of self- and object-representations, since the very events which would generally be the testing ground for one's sense of self (in this case social relationships during adolescence) cannot be experienced independently. Such independent experiencing would appear necessary in learning to gauge one's own strengths and weaknesses.

Perhaps the most poignant illustration of the feeling that one is not an individual but rather part of a unit is provided by Cindy as she described her feelings about the twinship:

"Like anyone talking or asking questions about it, about being twins, then I get the feeling about how much closer I am with her, and I have experiences with her that nobody else has—just between us."

Interviewer: "Can you describe that?"

Cindy: "I don't know, it's just like I have a fullness in my chest, and it's just like I am really happy. Sometimes it feels like if I keep talking about it, I just get really excited. 'My gosh!' Sometimes I don't understand it. 'Is it because I like the closeness, or what is it?' Sometimes I feel so happy about it that I don't know—I can't even compare it with anything. It's like a fullness, like I don't know, as if you have been empty or something, and you reached a peak and you feel full, *like a complete person.* I can't describe it" (my emphasis).

Cindy's is the most extreme depiction of this feeling that one is part of a unit. Furthermore, Cindy and Lindy were unusually close and involved with each other emotionally. In this sense, the sentiment described by Cindy here may not be typical.

In chapter 2 several examples were presented in which the members of a twinship dichotomized personality traits in a somewhat rigid manner. This polarization was often (though by no means exclusively) linked to stereotypic sex-role characteristics. Sandie, for example, was interested in art and literature, was more contemplative, and played with dolls as a child. Her sister Jean, on the other hand, had always preferred math and science courses, was more athletic, and was described as a tomboy while growing up. Similarly, in his twinship, Tom was more aesthetically oriented, was more domestically inclined, less athletic; whereas Tim was interested in art only as a form of investment, did not care about keeping their apartment orderly and clean, and was described as the "aggressive one," the "adventurous one" who was more of a "wolf" with women. Other twinships described here suggested similar dichotomizations (Charles and Frank, Henri and Ian, Christie and Kathy, Cindy and Lindy, among others). Such polarizations would appear to have a developmental function— namely, to create areas of expertise, domains of selfhood, through which the twins achieve a nonconflictual sense of themselves as different and unique. Sandie and Jean, for example, specifically noted that these differences made it possible for them to avoid competition with one another.

Like interdependence, this sort of polarization of identity characteristics is also a double-edged sword. On the one hand, such differentiation does provide for necessary areas of selfhood; it can become the mooring of a self-system, since it is around these distinguishing characteristics that one's sense of self becomes organized (this is probably best reflected in the consistency with which both twins used the same adjectives to describe each other). Yet, to the extent that such polarizations are rigid and somewhat forced, they can also undermine the very sense of identity that they are intended to insure.

Every family constellation represents a pool of personality characteristics that can potentially contribute to a child's own personality organization. Just how these available characteristics are used by the child in forming his or her own identity is not fully understood. However, the process would appear to involve varying degrees of identification with important people in the child's environment (see chapter 3), as well as other processes that are contingent on the nature of the interactions which evolve within a given family and on how the child understands these. It is likely that excessive rigidity in sorting through these experiences can distort the gradual process of consolidation of a sense of identity. For example, genuine potentials, talents, and interests might be relinquished in the service of maintaining a distinction between oneself and one's twin.

Debbie and Dianne provide a good illustration. In this twinship, Debbie had consistently been described as "the dumb one" during their childhood years. In fact, Debbie had done poorly in school in comparison to Dianne, who was considerably more studious. Debbie commented on this during the twins' joint interview: "In my mind Dianne was in a better position [in the family] because she was considered the smarter one. I was stronger but yet dumber."

Upon graduation from high school, Dianne went to a four-year university, while Debbie stayed at home and attended a local community college. But for reasons which never became clear during the interviews, these roles changed dramatically during the next two years. At the time of the interviews, Dianne had been out of school for two years, having dropped out after her sophomore year. Debbie had completed her studies at the junior college, had transferred to a prestigious university away from home, and was only a few weeks from graduation. During her individual interviews, Debbie described part of this process:

"I remember when the family used to call me 'dumb.' I keep referring back to this, I don't know why. I just have a need to talk about this intelligence issue. She [Dianne] used to call me 'dumbbell.' 'Dianne, can't you see that I'm not really dumb? Don't gang up on me with the rest of the family.'. . . she did that for years until finally I fought back. I said, 'I'm not dumb, don't you dare call me dumb again.'"

The difficulty involved in breaking away from that role was described by Debbie during the joint interview with Dianne, in the context of discussing her coming graduation from college. The twins were discussing their attempts to work out a greater degree of understanding in their relationship.

Debbie: "I'm graduating and Dianne has only gone to college two years, so it's really hard for me to keep checking this out with her, like saying, 'Does this kind of hurt your feelings?' or 'How do you feel about it, the fact that I'm graduating from college?'"

Interviewer: "How do you feel about it?"

Debbie: "I'm scared because my *role*—the way I looked at myself was the dumb one, and I ask myself, 'Does this mean I'm the smarter one now?' I'd like to think that way, but it's not healthy, and I don't want to think that way. I'm constantly trying to talk about it with Dianne, to check it out with her. The more I talk about it, the more I can face reality and not have to fantasize and try to put myself in the role of the smarter one."

The price paid in this role dichotomization is clarified by this illustration. The role of the dumb one was not only unpleasant, it was also inaccurate. It is possible that a key event which allowed Debbie to begin to question her assigned role in the family was Dianne's moving away to go to college. With Dianne gone, Debbie could venture into previously inaccessible domains of selfhood. In other words, it may be that twins mutually reinforce the polarized identity characteristics in each other. Yet it is clear from this illustration that breaking out of such a role is a difficult process. This is partly because even though Debbie may no longer feel that she is dumb, she continues to experience intelligence as a trait which *only one* of them can have. She must question whether her academic achievement has the effect of making *her* the "smart one" and relegating Dianne to the unpleasant role that Debbie had traditionally assumed in their family.

Various illustrations have been presented to show the effects of twinship on identity consolidation. These include an overt assumption that one's sense of self is tenuous or otherwise at risk, instances of marked dependency, and examples of rigid role differentiation. These issues appear to be interconnected. It is probably the case that close relationships always involve some degree of mutual dependency and interidentification (Kernberg, 1976). This is in the nature of intimacy. Further, it is not necessarily the case that these qualities always become manifested in nonadaptive ways. This was made particularly clear in two twinships, Darla and Marla and Debbie and Dianne, whose family environments were chaotic and conflict-ridden. The twin relationship, regardless of whatever other problems may have been associated with it, constituted a sanctuary for the twins from an otherwise unbearably stressful environment.

Darla and Marla's sister, for example, appears to have buckled under the stresses which characterized their family. She dropped out of high school, had become involved with drugs and was arrested, and was divorced and unable to take care of her children who periodically had to be taken in by relatives. The twins, too, appeared to have some difficulties. They had both been divorced, for example, and both seemed to have some problems in their personal lives. Yet both had attended college together, had apparently been socially successful there (Marla more than Darla), and had successfully completed advanced degrees. In other words, while the effects of a rather pathological family environment were not altogether neutralized by the twinship, the twins had clearly fared much better than their sibling.

The material presented in this chapter lends strong support to the conceptualizations presented in chapter 3. Many of the twenty-six twins who participated in this project are represented in this chapter. Further, these include identical, fraternal same-sex and fraternal opposite-sex twinships. While zygosity may affect a twin's experience in particular ways, it does not appear to be the overriding factor in considering how twinship affects development.

5

Adolescence and Adulthood

The main thrust of this book has centered on the early childhood of twins. The previous chapter, even though it contained material related to identity confusion in adolescent and adult twins, provided supportive evidence for the thesis that early child development and the twin situation in particular have an effect on twin psychological organization more generally. Because the twins in this study were mostly late adolescents and adults, their material offers an opportunity for a look at these points in the life cycle as well. This chapter examines the twin relationship beyond the childhood years from a number of vantage points, including the characteristics of twin development in adolescence and the fate of the twin relationship in adulthood.

Adolescence

Adolescence is frequently regarded as a period of developmental stress (e.g., Blos, 1967, 1970; Erikson, 1950, 1968; A. Freud, 1981). The various reasons include the adolescent's physiological maturation, increasing autonomy from the family, and changing relationships to peers. Erikson's (1950) description of this period as one in which the adolescent struggles to attain an "accrued confidence that the inner sameness and continuity prepared in the past are matched by the sameness and continuity of one's meaning for others" (p. 261) is an apt one. The chief task of adolescence, from a psychological perspective, is to consolidate the characteristics of one's psychological organization over the course of development with the skills developed during latency into a functional identity. Such an identity should enable the individual to emerge from adolescence with the capacity to act independently. During adolescence one must master conflicting feelings which center on a strong need to be regarded as a separate adult in command of one's own life, while experiencing feelings of anxiety regarding this process and the uncertainties which inevitably accompany it. Often, for the adolescent, the result is a "pushing away" and "holding on" to the family, like that seen in the earlier separation-individuation process which culminates at around thirty-six months of age (Blos, 1967). Blos emphasizes that this cyclical process serves to loosen the adolescent's infantile ties (i.e., it fosters differentiation), as part of the process of shedding family dependencies to become a member of the adult world. For these reasons adolescence has been referred to as the second separation-individuation (Blos, 1967).

For twins the adolescent period is particularly stressful, since a twin must often individuate not only from the family but also from the twin. In chapter 3 a rationale was proposed for why twins might turn to one another as special sources of comfort and support during separation-individuation. In chapter 4 several illustrations of this were presented in the form of the accentuated interdependency or interidentification evident in some twinships. Material suggesting that twins sometimes formed a unit that rallied against other family members might also be viewed as support for this formulation. Many twins presented such instances. Martha described the following: "[John] and I never argued between ourselves . . . we used to speak up for each other all the time [or] whenever there was a need for it. Inside our home, we teamed up against my sister."

Similarly, Melanie made this observation: "Margerie and I would always stick together . . . we used it to our advantage, especially against the boys [brothers]." A later comment by Melanie carries a similar implication although less overtly: "Margerie and I confided in each other and didn't tell mother a lot of things."

Vickie remembered the following: "He [brother] would just really do mean things to us—tease us, pull our hair. We would really get mad, so we would gang up on him and fight him."

These examples can be viewed as further illustrations of the difficulties in identity consolidation described in the previous chapter. They show the ways in which interdependence is accentuated by the twinship in the service of meeting external threats and challenges. While such interdependence may be helpful and comforting in the face of certain developmental stresses, it, too, becomes part of what the twin must face in the struggle to differentiate from the nuclear family during adolescence. By adolescence, these mechanisms are no longer functional in most twinships for a number of reasons. The most important is that in adolescence the peer group, rather than the family (including one's twin), normally becomes the center of activity. Prototypic adolescent situations—such as pairing up with a best friend with whom one has a special bond or behaviors that relate to the tremendous pressures to conform to a group standard to which one subjects his or her individuality (described by Erikson, 1968, as part of the transition from a family-dependent sense of self to a true "ego identity")—are remarkably like the twin situation in many respects. This very similarity may undermine the original "contract" which twins often make (if only implicitly) with one another. To develop a best friend outside of the twinship, for example, can raise questions regarding what should be shared with one's twin as opposed to one's friend. Is the secret divulged to a best friend a betrayal of the twinship? Or, to take a common adolescent concern, if one is more popular than one's twin, is that at the twin's expense? All of these issues suggest that adolescence would be particularly stressful for twins.

The twinships in this study fell into two general groups: those who had managed to differentiate from each other and those who had not. Among the former, adolescence often marked the onset of the differentiation process. The adolescence of these twins was characterized particularly by a feeling that the twin relationship had changed substantially during this period. The twins who described their adolescence as a significant crisis in the twin relationship and as a time when the twin relationship started to lose its all-encompassing, central role for them will be described first. These descriptions are followed by a look at twins who were able to postpone or prevent this dissolution of the twin relationship. In a later section of this chapter, dealing with the adult twin relationship, twins who appeared to be actively struggling with these issues at the time of the interviews will be discussed.

Margerie and Melanie are one set of twins for whom adolescence seems to have marked the beginning of a stormy period in their relationship. Margerie reported:

"This is an incident that I think we both recollect pretty clearly. We first really started having serious conflicts on a day-to-day basis when we were about eleven or twelve. We were in the sixth grade, and I can still remember this instance clearly because my mom made most of our clothes, and she just would make two of everything. We were dressed identically all the way through elementary school, and when we got to sixth grade, we started having huge fights every morning because I would want to wear one thing and she would want to wear something else. She wouldn't give in, and we would just have these big battles because I wouldn't give in either. I'd reached a point where I wasn't going to go along with that anymore."

Later Margerie added: "I think that probably when we got to our teen years we stopped being quite as close as we had been because we each, of course, developed our own interests in school. You get to pick courses. Melanie joined a few clubs, and I joined a few other clubs. I think that's probably when we stopped sharing every single thing."

Melanie dates the difficulties to a somewhat later period: "When we went to [college] as freshmen, that was really the first time we had any serious conflicts, especially about how each of us spent their time, and who they spent it with, and how money was spent. Because we shared a grocery allowance and stuff like that, that was the closest thing to really any fighting we ever did."

Melanie also mentioned that high school was a time when the twins were involved with different activities. Interestingly, Melanie's description that the twins stopped dressing alike in the sixth grade suggested that that event was much less momentous for her than it was for Margerie: "It dawned on us that we were always about the same size and that we would have a lot more changes of things if we didn't have to have two outfits exactly alike . . . so when we started junior high we quit dressing alike."

These major differences in perception in the events that twins experience as pivotal in their lives are interesting. Two points should be kept in mind regarding these discrepancies. First, the process of identity consolidation is dependent on the particulars of one's experience over time. In previous chapters an argument has been made that twin experiences over the course of development may be quiet different for each twin. For this reason, each twin might not always experience the *same* events as pivotal, since each twin is bringing different perceptions, expectations, and concerns to those developmental events. Second, because identity consolidation transpires over time, a broad range of events, rather than one or two, is likely to be important in that process. In some instances both twins may concur on the importance of an event, while in others, as in the illustration about dressing alike, they may not. In Melanie and Margerie's twinship, for example, both twins described going away to college as a period of considerable strain in their relationship (see chapter 4). Even then each twin had a different interpretation of what had actually happened during that time.

Debbie and Dianne showed reactions to different activities, which might reflect a growing distance from the twinship. The first example relates a degree of competition between the twins to attain a developmental milestone and the social implications which such an attainment carried with it.

Debbie discussed competition in the domain of sexuality: "In adolescence who was going to develop first or who was going to get their period first was a very important issue because the way we were taught, whoever gets their period first is a woman first. So which one of us was going to become a woman first, it was very important."

In their joint interview, the following interchange appeared to reflect Debbie's anxiety that Dianne's having a boyfriend would mean a loss of Dianne as a central figure in her life. This example again illustrates that the same developmental step—in this instance, getting a boyfriend—might not affect each twin in the same way:

Dianne: "Debbie had a lot of boyfriends way before I started dating at all, and it just really didn't bother me a lot. Then, when I got a boyfriend, she was real jealous about it."

Interviewer: "What happened?"

Debbie: (interjecting) "I would always spy on her, from my bedroom window. Those two would be out in the car making out, and they knew I was spying. I was very jealous. I didn't want anyone to steal Dianne away from me. *Dianne was mine!*"

Charles zeroed in on this same developmental period as a time of growing distance in his relationship to Frank: "Age thirteen, I'd say, puberty, had a lot to do with it. Our sexual awareness and things like that were real different. . . . By our senior year in high school we had drifted apart completely. By the time we could assert our physical independence, we were breaking apart slowly, dissolving the brotherhood, the twinship."

For Jean and Sandie, adolescence was clearly a time of difficulty:

Jean: "A lot of our friend pattern changed around going to junior high, but before that we really shared our friends pretty equally. We always went to the same person's house to play with friends, except for a few minor differences. In junior high that started to change."

Sandie: "When we were fifteen, sixteen, seventeen, we really had problems defining our relationship, what the nature of our intimacy was all about. For example, if you had best friends, were you expected to tell your twin everything, too?"

Like Debbie and Dianne, sexuality seemed to be a particularly stressful arena, at least for Jean. After being asked at the end of her first interview whether there was anything that she wanted to add, Jean said:

"I think that an important time in high school relationships was when Sandie got a boyfriend, because she got a boyfriend before I did. They went steady for about two years in high school. All of a sudden we wouldn't talk as much because she didn't want to share things about that relationship very much . . . I sort of felt closed out then. That was a hard time, that was a very hard time. I think that in our sharing experience, relations with guys really made our relationship a lot different."

In part what accentuated this period of crisis was that Sandie's newfound relationship became an area of privacy and of exclusion as far as Jean was concerned. In Jean's perception, Sandie did not confide in her about the new relationship. Jean described herself as quite hurt by Sandie's apparent lack of trust, she seemed perplexed as to the reasons for this secrecy:

Jean: "I remember that time as real traumatic—the thing was that she didn't seem to trust me, and I was like anybody else. She thought that, if she told me, I would go around and gossip. I just felt sort of left out and a little cheated that I didn't know what she was doing or how she felt about things."

As with Margerie and Melanie, Sandie and Jean had very different versions about this event, reflected in Sandie's depiction of it during her individual interviews:

"I have always felt guilty that we weren't closer. I've put the blame on myself—felt guilty. I don't know if Jean did [also]. Rationally, I don't think that I should feel like that. If it didn't work out naturally [their closeness], then you should not push it."

Interviewer: "When you feel guilty about it, have you ever thought about why you would be responsible for that?"

Sandie: "When we were fifteen, I didn't forgive her for something that she did that closed me off to her. I had the first boyfriend, and . . . he gave me a kiss, which I told her about. She had her circle of friends, and the next day at school they made some comment, and that hurt me. So I told her that I didn't like that, and I didn't confide in her anymore because it was the only way of keeping it private."

For Jean, these events sparked a major crisis in terms of the twin relationship: it implied change in the level of communication in the twinship and, perhaps, in the extent of Sandie's involvement with her more generally. To Jean, this change was of traumatic proportions for her—the first time in which she sensed the loss of the twin relationship as a special and exclusive entity.

In reality, this event appeared to be the culmination of a process that had started several years before. Jean described other events early in the twins' adolescence which were clearly the precursors of what we have just seen:

"Junior high school is sort of fuzzy to me. I started to meet kids from other junior high schools, and then some of it happened over the summer. But a lot more [happened] in the first year of high school [when Sandie started going out with her boyfriend]. We were like best friends in elementary school, and then in junior high we each got some of our own friends and sort of got into different activities a little bit. But we still talked about everything we did, and we would still. I don't remember when exactly, but there was a time in there, seventh or eighth grade, when we got separate rooms. But we would take turns going into each other's room at night and talking before we would go to bed; [we would] rehash everything that had happened during the day."

Interviewer: "So actually in a number of ways adolescence was kind of a major shift. What gives it that traumatic quality?"

Jean: "I don't think that the separate rooms or anything was traumatic. I liked that, I think, [but] the lack, the change in communication and the change in sharing *was* traumatic."

Although Sandie described the events involving her boyfriend also as having pulled her away from Jean, her reaction does not have the momentous impact on Sandie's psychological life that it does on Jean's. As with Margerie and Melanie and Debbie and Dianne, Jean and Sandie have different views of the same events. They also placed different emphases on which events were pivotal in fostering or precipitating a greater degree of differentiation within the twinship. For Sandie, this awareness had also come during their adolescence, but a year or so earlier.

In describing various childhood illnesses which the twins had suffered together and how supportive they had been to one another during these illnesses, Sandie mentioned a major physical problem which had not been shared:

Sandie: "In high school . . . I had to wear a back brace for curvature of the spine, which is hereditary. But Jean didn't have it badly [describes the brace]. It influenced my behavior; it made me more introspective and self-conscious. I became quieter."

Interviewer: "What was that like?"

Sandie: "It was frightening . . . also there was a sense that it wasn't fair, that it was a *twin problem* that *I* had to get over. It was a hereditary disease, and I couldn't understand why. I kept thinking that it would be easier if both of us had to do it at the same time, because there had been other things, like getting tonsils taken out, and chicken pox . . . things we had gone through at the same time, we had always done together. But this time I had to do it by myself. This was the first painful thing that I had to do by myself. I resented it a lot because the reason why we went [to the doctor] in the first place was because Jean had bad posture, and mother was concerned. The doctor said, 'Now that Sandie is here, we might as well check her too.' And the result was, 'Well, Sandie has beautiful posture, but a bad back.' And I felt that it was tremendously unfair . . . and it was harder because someone had escaped it [haltingly]. Rationally I am glad that she escaped it, especially now that I am over it, but irrationally I felt, 'It isn't fair!'"

Interviewer: "So how did you feel about that?"

Sandie: "I just remember that day that I came back from the doctor . . . and I sat in Jean's room . . . the room we both had had. I sat there by myself and cried in her room, on my old bed, rather than in my new room. I realized that she wasn't there on the other side . . . and there was a real sense of being alone."

The realization that the other bed was empty and that Sandie was there by herself reflects a deep sense of longing for the comfort and succor of the twinship. This material poignantly accentuates the singular importance of Jean in Sandie's life and is further support for the formulations presented in chapters 3 and 4 regarding the soothing or comforting (transitional) function of the twin relationship. From Sandie's perspective this event appears to have driven a wedge between herself and Jean. (Interesting, Jean made no mention of this event during her interviews.) Having to experience this by herself altered Sandie's experience of the twin relationship in a profound way, which she found difficult to articulate but which is captured by the feeling of being extremely alone while sitting on the bed. For Sandie, the sense of separateness was already a living reality prior to her finding an intimate relationship outside of the twinship.

Adulthood

The material on adolescence illustrates the manner in which, for some twinships, this period poses major psychological stress. This was not the case in all twinships, however. For some twins, it was later adolescence, especially leaving home together for the first time—going away to college, for example—that precipitated the same sorts of crises which have just been illustrated. These twinships are discussed in terms of the twin relationship in adulthood, since, in effect, theirs seemed to either postpone the adolescent issues or prolong them into late adolescence (eighteen or nineteen years of age) and early adulthood.

There seemed to be considerable variation in the relationships that adult twins maintained with each other. One cluster of twinships seemed to be very much involved with one another. For instance, for several twinships who were in their late teens or early twenties, their lives were still interconnected. Vicky and Valery would be one such example. In their first year of college, these twins shared an apartment, were involved in the same social groups, took classes together, and even continued to dress alike with some frequency. Cindy and Lindy were also in a similar position and of the same age. Although they did not share a dormitory room at college because of a clerical error, they had fully expected to. They, too, were involved in the same social groups—being rushed by the same sorority, for example. They shared a best friend. With few exceptions, Cindy and Lindy were taking the same classes in college. In these two twinships, then, while life had brought them into contact with the fact of separation (see discussion of Cindy and Lindy in chapter 4), they were still actively involved with one another and had only just begun to grapple with the issues of separation and differentiation which inevitably faced them.

The same issues remained for some of the older twin pairs. Tim and Tom, for example, in their mid-twenties, still shared an apartment, worked at the same office, and for the most part were socially involved with the same friends. Henri and Ian, in their late forties, had in recent years attained a greater degree of differentiation in their lives. They now lived in different cities—both were teachers, although they taught different subjects. However, until their early forties, Henri and Ian had been members of the same religious order, after having attended college together. Presumably their involvement in the religious order meant, among other things, that the twins had occasionally continued to dress alike until they were in middle age. In short, their lives had been greatly intertwined until recent years. Fred and Ted, in their mid-thirties, were also involved in each other's lives. Both twins taught at the same university in the same department, while sharing a private practice outside the university. They were involved in intramural sports and played on the same teams together. The twins occasionally took vacations together as well, with and without their families. These twinships would epitomize the closest relationships which were found in this group of twins in adulthood.

In a second group, the twinships appeared to be at different phases of coming to terms with separation. These twins seemed to be in the midst of this process. For example, during the eighteen months prior to their interviews, Melissa and Stephanie had begun experimenting with being apart. This had included going to different colleges (although within fifteen miles of one another), each twin living in her own apartment. After taking a trip to Europe together, however, the twins moved back home. Just prior to the interviews, Melissa had moved out on her own, while Stephanie had remained at home. This move had created considerable tension between the twins. (When asked how her leaving home had affected her relationship with Stephanie, Melissa exclaimed, "Oh! That's a sore subject!") Thus, Melissa and Stephanie appeared to be in the middle of negotiating this difficult period in their relationship.

Earlier in this chapter, material relating to the adolescent onset of separation issues in the Margerie-Melanie twinship were discussed. In fact, these twins continued to grapple with these difficulties at the age of thirty. In chapter 4, Margerie described the tensions of the twin relationship when they first went to college. These tensions were engendered by Melanie's relationship with her boyfriend, since this involvement had meant that Margerie was excluded a great deal from activities that she might otherwise have done with Melanie. The twins reached a moratorium of sorts that lasted several years after this difficult period. During that time, when both twins were married, the two couples spent considerable time together as a foursome. When Margerie divorced her husband, Melanie noted that in addition to her concern for Margerie in this difficult period, she and her husband also felt it to be a major loss to themselves, since the two couples had once spent nearly half of their time together. Although Margerie moved in with Melanie and her husband for a period of several months after her divorce, she soon moved out and, for the first time, lived by herself. When Margerie remarried several years later, the closeness of the original foursome was never reestablished. A social network which had served the function of keeping the twins highly involved with one another was, in effect, dissolved.

Since then, Margerie has gone about establishing an independent life for herself. At the time of the interviews it was clear that she was actively trying to alter the remnants of what she considered a problematic relationship with her twin sister in which Melanie seemed to want to be more involved with Margerie's life than was comfortable for Margerie. Melanie did not seem to have the same sense about the relationship. Thus, this twinship was undergoing major changes in the nature of the twin relationship—changes that had clearly been in the making for some time. They had begun early in adolescence, had become accentuated when first going to college, had subsided for a period of years during Margerie's first marriage, and had finally reemerged decisively after Margerie's divorce.

A final group of twins were now leading fairly separate lives. The contact between them did not seem very different from that found among other family members. However, the amount of actual differentiation from the twinship, as opposed to overt differentiation, varied within this group. The distinction is an important one. A few twins, while leading lives which were quite different from one another, still appeared to be preoccupied with the twinship or actively invested in it psychologically, in spite of the appearances to the contrary. It is also the case that the manifest interrelationship between twins is not *necessarily* the best measure of the degree of differentiation in a psychological sense. For example, although Henri and Ian had spent a considerable part of their lives very much involved with one another, theirs did not appear to be an interdependence that interfered with their lives.

One example of a twinship that had attained a considerable degree of overt differentiation, while remaining tied psychologically, was that of Darla and Marla. Darla and her sister lived in different cities, had different careers, and saw one another only once or twice a year. Both twins were now divorced, although this had been a twinship in which the twins and their spouses had spent a great deal of time together as a foursome (for example, they had traveled extensively together). The failure of their marriages as well as other life events (such as choosing different careers) had separated them geographically and had created major differences in their activities. Yet Darla was still very involved in the twinship and in the meaning of her relationship with Marla.

There were ways in which the twinship had really kept Darla afloat, psychologically, during her divorce:

"It was a hard summer when [ex-husband] left, and Marla was one of the things that pulled me through that summer. . . . My relationship with Marla has been getting better and changing. She's always been there, and I just sort of pushed it [the relationship] back, and I'm never going to do this again. I feel strongly about that now, because when I really needed help—I mean I was just devastated—it was Marla who was always there. She paid my way to go out to see her . . . I was emotionally starving [with ex-husband]. I wanted someone to need me very badly, and I think maybe that's one of the things that Marla helped me with, because she does need me, and she does care about me."

Yet, the current relationship was not as ideal as this description would seem to indicate. For example, during a recent visit, Darla reported: "We spent a week together, and she was going to go have dinner with some friends, and she wanted me to come. I just said, 'Marla, wouldn't you really rather go alone?' She said, 'Well, Darla, to be really honest, I would rather go alone, but it's fine if you come.' And I said, 'Marla, I don't want to go because I need time to myself, and I think you do too.' [So] she went alone."

At times Darla's sense of self continued to be contingent upon what happened in this relationship, and the integration of her sense of self was tenuous. Although externally Marla and Darla seemed to be differentiated, Darla's inner feelings about herself and her twin suggested a different picture. Separation-individuation is not, after all, a physical process as much as it is a psychological one. The adequacy of the intrapsychic differentiation is most important, not the external particulars. Darla was actually frightened of being in the same place with Marla for too long because of the effects of such contact on her sense of self and her self-esteem.

Debbie and Dianne were in a similar position. They lived in different cities, although they had periodic contact. Overtly, their lives were different. Debbie was graduating from college; Dianne was a college dropout. Debbie had what might be described as solidly middle-class values and aspirations, while Dianne lived a decidedly counterculture life-style. Debbie hoped soon to marry her fiancé. Dianne considered herself a radical feminist and had major reservations about heterosexuality. Yet, as seen in chapter 4, these twins felt actively involved in trying to sort out the nature of their relationship and what it meant to them. The relationship remained conflictual; and, despite the differences and geographic distance, the twinship continued to exert a considerable psychological influence on each. For example, consider Debbie's guilt and anxiety about graduating from college (described in chapter 4) in which it is clear that Dianne's perceptions of her still affected Debbie greatly in important areas of her life.

The following quotation reflects the extent to which Dianne and Debbie were actively attempting to negotiate their relationship in the present:

Dianne: "The older we get, we're trying to work out things like that [competition] and let go of the competition and the comparing. We don't feel that it's healthy, and we don't feel that it's good for our relationship or growthful for us as individuals. We're trying to be more accepting of each other's life-styles and say, 'You're good at this and you're good at that' and [know] that they are not on the same scale and to be more cooperative with each other and to appreciate what each other can do without being competitive about it."

In both of these twinships, the fact that they were twins appears to have played an important role in their lives, as they reflected on the question, "How has being a twin affected your life?"

Darla gave this response: "I would have to say that being a twin has probably influenced—has been the single most significant influence in my life. I don't know if Marla and I are exceptional in thinking that way about it or not. We've always been real close . . . I think we have a real special relationship."

In response to the same question, Debbie said: "Almost every aspect of my life [has been affected]. Everything, really. Everything I do, every time I had some kind of achievement or loss or failing or anything, I always think about it in terms of *us*."

In these examples, the twins are overtly leading very different lives, but the fact of twinship continues to exert a considerable amount of influence psychologically. With other twinships, however, this pattern did not seem to be present. In them, the twins seemed to have attained a fair amount of differentiation. Whatever difficulties the process of differentiation from their twin had created were now behind them, for the most part. Jean and Sandie would be an example of one such twinship. They lived in the same city and had periodic contact with each other. While there continued to be areas of dissatisfaction with their relationship, the twins apparently arrived at a mutual understanding of the nature and limits of their relationship.

One striking feature in many twinships was that the twins seemed to be differentially invested in the relationship. In these instances, one twin appeared more committed and involved, while the other was more disengaged, more willing to deemphasize their twinness, or more willing to go beyond the twinship for important social needs.

For example, Margerie described the following feelings about her relationship with her twin sister, discussing her sense that in many ways they have gone their separate ways socially and in career choice.

Margerie: "We have totally different careers, our circle of friend here in [city where she lives] doesn't even overlap at all. She know some of my friends. She's met them at parties and things like that, bu she never sees them any other time except when I invite her over t share my friends with her, so they don't really mesh at all. We move i different circles and don't really have a lot in common except that we're sisters."

Margerie added: [Melanie] tries to get me to participate in he interests and injects herself into mine to a greater extent than I feel is necessary for us to remain close. She'll invite several of her friends ove to her house and . . . she'll want [Margerie's husband] and me to come and spend a great deal of time with her friends. This is at least weekly that she comes up with these ideas, but we don't have anything in common with her friends except that she knows them and we know her. They usually come from different career fields than we have in common, and it's real hard for her to understand. In fact she gets mad when I don't want to come all the time and insists that I come. She often calls up and insists that I cancel other plans to come and share her friends. On one plane it's wrong for me to say, 'No, I'm not going to do that.' On another plane—this is something I've just begun to realize lately—it seems that that is perhaps not her only goal. It's not all just because she cares about me and she wants to share her friends with me because she cares about me, but it has a lot of other aspects of that domineering thing. She feels, I believe, that she's losing control. She doesn't any longer control my life."

Finally, Margerie links these issues directly to the differential investment in the twinship: "One of the things that was real interesting about our twinship is that I think she spends a whole lot more time aware of it—aware of the fact that she's a twin—than I do. A lot of my friends don't even know that I'm a twin. [Gives example of when it came up in a recent conversation with friends that she was a twin.] And those people I've known for a long time, two or three years, and they didn't even know that I was a twin. Whereas, with Melanie, every one of her friends that I meet knows already that I'm her twin when I meet them. . . . So I think for *her*, twinship is still very much something that's in the front of her mind . . . I think it sort of emphasizes what I'm saying about her approach to our relationship."

Vickie described similar differences in her relationship with Valery in discussing their adolescence: "There was one time at the beginning of high school when I wanted to be twins more than she did. It really didn't matter to her if we dressed alike or not. A lot of times we dressed differently because she would get dressed, and I didn't want to wear that. Well, she wouldn't compromise, and so we would dress differently. I remember that she didn't really care that much about us being twins. We weren't fighting or anything, but just at that time she didn't care. . . . Mother would say, 'Vickie demands more about the twinship than Valery does.'"

Debbie and Dianne from their joint interview:

Debbie: "I remember that ma tried to dress us alike."

Dianne: "She asked us if we wanted to be and she kind of wanted us to, but you said, 'No,' and I wanted to [dress alike]."

Debbie: "I never wanted to because I hated the comparison all the time. It felt good to me to be a separate way from Dianne."

In some twinships these differences in investment appeared clearly during the joint interviews in the way in which the twins interacted or in the positions that they took. There seemed to be a covert, although sometimes overt, protest against the very notion of twinness. In the following example, Tim seems to emphasize the differences between himself and Tom, while Tom attempts to obscure them:

Tim: "No one has ever tested us to see if we're identicals, so we're not sure if we're fraternal twins who look so much alike, look like brothers, or whether we're twins. He [pointing to Tom] looks like our mother's side of the family . . ."

Tom: (interrupting) "Well, you do too, like some cousins and stuff!"

Tim: "But I have a more fuller face, and everyone who sees us together mentions . . ."

Tom: (again interrupting) "Well! You can be identical and still have . . . I don't know what you'd call it, a little . . . carry more [last name] gene or something."

Tim: "No, because then you wouldn't be identical. [To interviewer] identical means what, same egg? two sperm? Right?"

Interviewer: "One egg . . ."

Tim: "That splits apart . . ."

Tom: (ostensibly changing the topic) "When we were little . . ."

Tim: (interrupting) "Show him the picture."

Tom: "Tim was going to say we were Siamese twins who were separated."

Tim: (laughs and emphatically adds) "And separated! [They show interviewer the picture] Can you pick us out? You should be able to because many of the characteristics which we have today are present. [Interviewer picks wrong.] No! Wrong! I'll tell you why now . . . because I'm always the more solemn one. Tom always gets a big laugh on his face!"

Tom: "A cheerful baby!"

In this good-natured exchange Tim consistently emphasizes the qualities that distinguish the twins. In reality the twins were exceedingly similar in appearance. Co-workers frequently got them confused to the extent that on occasion the twins *functioned* in each other's stead rather than correct confused colleagues. Their girl friends were not able to distinguish their voices on the telephone. Tim and Tom presented many such examples during the course of their interviews. Through this emphasis on differences, Tim implicitly distanced himself from the twinship itself and its connotations of close similarity.

Steve and Amy recapitulated this theme in their joint interview. Steve underscored his separateness from his sister and deemphasized his relationship to her. In fact, when I initially contacted him and asked if he might be interested in participating in the study, Steve had responded that he would be glad to take part, suggesting, however, that it might be a waste of my time, since he hardly thought of himself as a twin. This stance is accentuated in the joint interview:

Amy: "For a long time I thought that Steve didn't want people to know that we were twins. I don't know if that was told to me or what. I don't remember it" (spoken in a conciliatory tone, directed as much at Steve as to the interviewer).

Steve: "Well, you used to go around telling people we were twins and I didn't . . . because it didn't matter to me."

Amy: "I still do! Like when I introduced Steve . . . to me it's always been a novelty."

Interviewer: (to Steve) "Did you downplay it?"

Steve: "I don't know how it ever came up . . . [maybe] in introductions . . . and I never introduce people. If I did introduce Amy I would say, 'my sister,' she'd say, 'my twin brother.' Amy made certain that people knew."

At another juncture in the same interview Amy stated: "Steve and I were in spelling bees. It seemed we would always get out right at the same time, almost the same word! We were good at it, too!"

Steve: "I remember getting out, but I don't remember how you would do."

Still later in the same interview the following exchange took place:

Interviewer: "Has being twins affected your lives?"

Steve: "Basically I haven't thought of it . . . it's difficult to answer that. There are specific incidents that have occurred that I remember, that related directly to being a twin . . ."

Amy: (interrupting, a sense of surprise and excitement in her voice) "Really? Like what?"

Steve: "Like dad saying, 'Treat your sister nice, she's your twin,' that kind of thing."

Amy: (dejectedly) "Yeah. Yeah."

Steve: "But the fact is that I never treated you poorly because you were my twin, so why should I treat you nicely because you are my twin?"

And finally, Amy: "I would read the Bobsey twins and I'd always, of course, imagine that it was me and my brother Steve, idealized. It was a family with two sets of twins, two boys and two girls . . ."

Steve: (interrupting) "I never read the stuff."

In a manner that was decidedly less playful in character than Tim and Tom's example, Steve consistently rebuffed Amy's efforts to cast the twinship in a warm glow. Her wish to accentuate the twinship and enlist him in a shared fantasy of closeness ("it seemed we would always get out . . . right at the same time, almost at the same word") was matched by Steve's disappointing lack of interest in her overtures ("I never read the stuff").

Many of the twins who were involved in this project manifested similar differential investments in the twin relationship itself. The sources for such differential investment were not always evident but are no doubt quite complex. One might speculate that it comes from such key developmental events as differential relationships with each of the parents. For example, in instances where one twin has a more optimal attachment to the mother, such a twin might have developed a more cohesive sense of self, resulting in greater felt security in functioning independently of the twinship. The co-twin, under these circumstances, might still feel incomplete without the twin, resulting in greater efforts to maintain the relationship. In other twinships it may be that differential masculine and feminine identifications (see chapter 4) are responsible for the noted differences in investment in the relationship. In this instance, the "masculine" twin may feel compelled to disavow the twinship insofar as the attachment to the twin is experienced as an identity-threatening, "feminine" feeling, while the co-twin is more comfortable expressing feelings of warmth and closeness. Thus, as one considers the basis for a differential investment in the twin relationship, one must exert caution in making assumptions about underlying personality structure on the basis of overt behavior.

Perceptions about Twinship

The last portion of this chapter examines different perceptions that twins have about the nature of twin relationships in general and the extent to which their own relationship conforms to these preconceptions about twinship. Across the ages, twinship has had a strong psychological impact on others. This is reflected in mythology and folklore as well as in scientific literature. Though perhaps somewhat less magically, twinship continues to have a similar effect. For example, the descriptions by many twins of going to public places together were in ways reminiscent of the lives of celebrities. Similarly, mothers of twins consistently remarked on the attention, curiosity, and interest that their twins provoked in public places. Twinship is commonly perceived as being a uniquely close relationship, at times bordering on the supernatural, characterized by a special level of communicativeness and commitment to one another. Twins are by no means unaffected by beliefs such as these. In fact, they frequently identify with them strongly. Thus, it is not surprising to find that twins often characterize twinship in the same idealizing manner that nontwins do.

Various theorists have attempted to account for the reactions that twinship precipitates in others and for the sources of the mythology surrounding twinship. Largely, these accounts center on the notion that, through the ambiguity surrounding their identity, twins somehow challenge our own identities. There is something universally appealing and fascinating about the loss of individual boundaries (Burlingham, 1946, 1952; Joseph, 1961). In terms outlined by Mahler et al. (1975), this phenomenon can be understood as reflecting a wish to return to a symbiotic relationship—that is, a relationship characterized by a lack of self-object differentiation in which one's needs are magically understood and met. Many of the twins who participated in this study described instances of special understanding or empathy between them.

Melissa and Stephanie, for example, said that at times they could communicate in incomplete sentences and still know what the other was saying:

Stephanie: "Something that happens when we are traveling together, we can be thinking about the same thing, and—only one person will get it out of their system first—like a split second before the other person does. We can even talk in incomplete sentences and know fully what we are talking about."

Melissa: (interjecting an example) "A long time ago we'd go to concerts, and Stephanie would say, 'Look at the lady with the orange shirt,' and there would be no one around like that, but I would know what she was talking about."

Tim and Tom had a special word for this phenomenon—a "mite": "I am thinking of Tom making something, like: 'Gee I am hungry; I wish Tom were making cornbread or brownies,' and sometimes he is out there already making it, or wishing that we had some ice cream or something, and Tom's in the kitchen getting out the ice cream already."

Although Tim and Tom discussed this as though it were a twin phenomenon, in fact, it turned out that "mites" were a family affair: "We have a saying in our family: 'mites.' When someone does something that you are thinking about—like if I want Tom to do something and he does it before I say anything."

Noteworthy about these examples (which were typical) is that, in fact, they are not unusual. Tim and Tom note that "mites" are a family rather than exclusively a twin phenomenon. However, they do capture the uniqueness which the twins believe characterizes their relationships. The subjects in this study often contrasted the twin relationship to nontwin sibships, thereby frequently articulating an ideal view of what being a twin is. Through such depictions it is possible to see in relief the feeling that twinship is a special and uniquely close relationship.

For example, Debbie described the following special bond between herself and Dianne, which she feels is deeper than bonds that she has with others in her family.

Debbie: "There was a bond there . . . that she really understood what I was feeling, almost as if she was a part of me."

Interviewer: "What does that feel like?"

Debbie: "Good. Good. It's very secure and very nice. My other family members, I'm kind of close to them, but Dianne, there is a much closer bond there . . . that's one of the really lucky aspects of being a twin."

The following material from other twins reflects a similar point of view regarding the specialness of the twin relationship:

Cindy: "I feel closer to [Lindy] because it just seems like I am closer to her than other people are and closer to her than regular siblings would be, sisters and brothers, and by talking about it I realize how much closer I am to her than other people."

Tom: "Being a twin isn't the same as being a close brother or sister, even one year younger or older or something—it's nice being a twin—always someone around."

Martha: "He [her husband] has come to accept that he can never understand our [twin] relationship. He couldn't understand the difference between being a twin and being a brother and sister, only he knew there was a difference between the way we related to one another."

Interviewer: "How did you relate to one another?"

Martha: "Like the fact that we never argued. He's seen my brother and me around other members of my family; he's seen us pick on the other siblings—so the quality of our relationship is different between twins and brothers."

A friend of one set of twins also accentuated this theme: "She said, 'You know, people are going to notice you more than just brothers and sisters,' and I did notice that it fascinates people to see twins."

As this material reflects, many twins clearly subscribe to what we might call a utopian view of twinship—that is, twinship viewed as a personification or embodiment of a unique closeness. Indeed it seems that in many respects twins *are* quite close. Further, many of the twins who offered these idealized perspectives on the twin relationship presented direct memories and experiences attesting to that closeness. However, another view of the twin relationship was prevalent among the twins who participated in the study. In spite of the more positive memories, a pervasive sense emerged that the twins' *own* relationship did not actually constitute an instance of the special closeness just described. Instead, these twins seemed to view themselves as *exceptions* to the twin relational perfection to which they, themselves, subscribed as a general reality. Note that many of the twins cited below were the same twins who depicted the utopian view described before. There is a certain poignancy to these accounts, since one witnesses a degree of disappointment as these twins reflect on their relationship and contrast it to what they think "real" twin relationships should be.

Amy: "He [Steve] thought of me as his sister rather than his twin."

Tim: "I think that after we were split up [in fourth grade] he was more just like a brother. I knew that we were twins, of course, but I began to look at him more, just [like] a brother."

In his final interview Tim returned to this same view: "Like I said before, I don't look at Tom as a twin, but more so as a brother, sibling maybe, just a brother. Because we were separated in school, we weren't as close as two twins might be if they were in the same grade and were constant companions. As a result of our being split up, I look on him more like a brother."

During his own interviews Tom independently reflected the same viewpoint: "We do a lot together, but we live our own lives—so as far as that goes, we are probably more like brothers than like twins. We do things that normal brothers do."

This underscores a dual view of twinship. On the one hand, some of these twins articulate an ideal fantasy of twinship, of the specialness of this relationship. On the other, they suggest a sense of dislocation. They seem to feel that they themselves have become disconnected from that utopia. In other words, the contrast that these twins make between twins and normal brothers is a version of the utopian view of twinship, even though these twins see themselves as exceptions to that ideal. With Tim, in particular, there is a feeling of missed opportunity. The sense of a closeness which has been lost is quite prominent. Before being separated, they were like *real* twins, now they are more like just plain brothers.

In spite of the level of intensity of the twin relationship which has been illustrated in this and other chapters, there is a sense in which twins are not really as close as twins and nontwins seem to believe. The following material offers a clearer illustration. If the utopian characterization of the twin relationship is understood as a mythology of sorts, then these examples accentuate the tragic quality of such a distortion. Many of these twin subjects characterized *their own* twin relationships as having some distance and lacking communication. For example, this is how Amy began her individual interviews following the joint interview:

Interviewer: "I want to ask you what your reactions were [to the joint interview]."

Amy: "I really enjoyed the two of us—I appreciate the two of us being in the same room together, discussing our childhood and the fact that we're twins, because actually we don't talk about things."

Tom captures a similar feeling in their relationship in the context of discussing why he and Tim are not all that close:

Interviewer: "Do you ever feel sad about that?"

Tom: "No, I am sure over the years there are things that could have been different, but that's the way it turned out, you just have to accept it."

Interviewer: "What could have been different?"

Tom: "Well, we don't confide in each other, and the things we do, problems or anything, we talk to others about them [but not to each other]. We try to get away from being too dependent on each other as much as possible. We try to live our own lives, so we get to know each other, but we don't get to know all of the intimate details or anything."

Interviewer: "Do you sometimes wish that you did?"

Tom: "Yes, but when you realize that that kind of communication isn't there and that there is nothing that you can do about it, you just let it slide by and don't worry about it. I try to worry about as few things as possible."

Tim: "I look at him [Tom] more like a brother—I mean, we're not so close that our innermost secrets are shared or anything like that. I told you that sometimes we don't talk about some things we do, so I look at him more like just a brother."

Tim returned to this theme during another interview: "There are still some things that we don't talk about—like sex—with each other, we were brought up and some things—we just can't talk about openly in our family. We can talk about it with friends and stuff, but together we don't talk about it—we don't talk about each other's experiences. If you don't talk about it, the other one doesn't know anything about it."

Martha finds it equally difficult to talk to her brother about her feelings regarding his marriage (described in chapter 4), a major event in her life which still preoccupies her, although it took place several years ago.

Interviewer: "Do you ever talk to him about this?"

Martha: "No! [sharply] I don't think that I could, I don't think that I would want to."

Interviewer: "Why not?"

Martha: "He and I have not really talked about things that are emotionally related, and it's probably due to the fact that both of us can become very emotional, and it would be difficult to handle. I would end up in tears, and he too. Part of me doesn't want him to know that I resent in any way that he got married."

Fred has a similar complaint: "By the nature of the way in which we were raised, we're close physically, but not personally. Our parents never taught us to express our feelings. Maybe that's why we get along so well, because we don't get involved to a great degree in our personal lives. If I am having problems with my wife, I don't sit down and talk to my brother about them."

Charles: (discussing his sense of loneliness and the wish that he had a friend with whom he could share interests and activities) "It's the same thing with Frank; I wish that I had something, that there was a relationship that we could share as twins. There is not much that Frank and I can get along with, because in everything that he does he tends to not necessarily pollute it but adds a little bit too much of himself into it."

Melissa: (in the context of discussing things that she doesn't tell Stephanie) "I'll just say, 'Forget it, I won't tell you.' Because I don't have to answer to her anymore." (regarding Stephanie's difficulty in finding a boyfriend) "We never talk about why her relationships don't last long."

Margerie: (regarding a recent conflict with Melanie in which Margerie did not want to spend a holiday with Melanie and her husband)

"She kept inviting me [and] I knew that her feelings would be very badly hurt if I told her honestly that that's not how I want to spend Thanksgiving, and I think it's a dumb idea. I couldn't be honest with her, so it's slowly eating away at the closeness of our relationship. Because I can't be close with her anymore, I can't say what I really think. I feel like we should be able to, if we are to live close and if we really matter to each other."

It is clear from the following material that these stresses in Margerie and Melanie's relationship were not new.

Interviewer: "I wondered what puberty was like for you."

Margerie: "I couldn't talk to my mother about it at all. It was just something that she had never tried to talk to me about. I talked about it with my sister [Melanie], and this is a strong memory of that time. Melanie started her period before I did, and she didn't tell me; she didn't talk about it with me at all. Then when my period started, and I told her about it, she helped me and she talked to me about it, but it was never in very personal terms—what it was like emotionally or whether we liked it or not. It was more like we talked about the mechanics of dealing with it, but not really whether we liked it or not [or] anything like that."

In this material it is possible to see the twin relationship in terms which are less idealized. Rather, twins are often participants in a relationship in which they are unable to communicate about what is most important to them. This material shows that twins encounter the same difficulties in human relationship as nontwins do. However, it is important to emphasize that this reality, in the context of the twin relationship, has different implications. Twins *expect* that their relationship should be special in this way, just as others often believe that the twin relationship is characterized by this special closeness (Burlingham, 1946). With accentuated expectations by twins and nontwins alike, being like normal brothers and sisters can be disappointing.

Various dimensions of the twin relationship during adolescence and adulthood have been presented. Adolescence appears to be a point of considerable stress for many twinships because the developmental tasks at hand bring powerful individuating pressures to bear on the relationship. This is made doubly difficult when the adolescent twin must negotiate a degree of separation and differentiation from the twin *at the same time* that these issues are being tested in the parent-child relationship. For many twins this seems to be the point where the twinship is "given up" as a primary relationship around which one must organize oneself. For others, sometimes after initially testing the ground, the twins seem to reconsolidate their relationship, although possibly on different terms. This seems to be what occurred in the Margerie-Melanie twinship, for example. Here, a moratorium on the process of differentiation from one's twin sets in. As seen in this same twinship, the ensuing ten years appeared to be characterized by a cycle of differentiation and de-differentiation. Such cases emphasize that in some twinships the process of differentiation gradually unfolds.

Adult twins were characterized by varying degrees of overt closeness and interdependence. However, care is required in assessing the meaning of this interweaving of lives. What is important is the degree of intrapsychic differentiation between twins, not whether they have an overtly close relationship. Failure to appreciate this fact leads to a potential for seeing pathology in a twinship where the siblings are simply close. To the extent that the twin relationship leads to interference in adequate functioning, be it in the realm of interpersonal relationships or in the capacity to attain realistic goals, concern about the intertwin relationship is warranted. However, twins should not be deprived of the opportunity of forming a close and lasting bond because of confusion between interpersonal closeness and distorted development. Finally, twins do not necessarily fit a utopian characterization of human relationships. This, too, is an important observation. To the extent that twins (or others) *expect* that from their relationship, it is likely that they will be disappointed.

6

Some Sources of Differentiation in Twinship

The extent of overt differentiation that one should attain from one's twin is a lifelong question with which twins must continually struggle. It is also a double-edged sword in twinship. On the one hand, the degree of attained differentiation between twins is sometimes taken as a measure of their normality and can thus become a goal which is imposed internally by the twins themselves as well as externally by those around them. On the other hand, insofar as intertwin differentiation is governed by these internally and externally derived pressures, there exists a danger of creating somewhat arbitrary points of demarcation in which some potentialities are relinquished, while others are appropriated. In this way, pressures to differentiate may help undermine the sense of identity that differentiation is supposed to safeguard.

In the present context *differentiation* is being used to refer to overt and manifest differences in characteristics and traits. This is different from the separation-individuation process described in chapters 3 and 5, in which the attainment of adequately differentiated self- and object-representations was discussed. The latter developmental milestone, which is intimately related to the consolidation of a cohesive sense of identity, is an internal psychological process whose overt behavioral manifestations are difficult to pinpoint. They may not necessarily be tied to the sorts of differences being discussed in this chapter. For example, as suggested in chapters 4 and 5, some twins may need to overaccentuate their differences in order to maintain a sense of themselves as separate individuals. Other twins, secure in their identities, may be able to develop a close and enduring relationship with one another which is not based on excessive dependence and a loss of self-object boundaries. Thus, the degree of overt differences between twins is a poor indicator of the extent to which twins have been successful in consolidating a firmly grounded sense of self.

In this chapter, two specific factors which contribute to the differentiation between twins are discussed. The first is the role of differential identifications with each of the twins' parents, discussed briefly in chapter 2. The second is the role of competition in the twinship. These factors were selected primarily because they were frequently discussed by subjects. In addition, competition is often cited in the clinical literature on twins. Thus, an examination of this dimension also helps clarify the role it plays in twin relationships.

Differential Parent Identifications

In his discussion of twin development, Lytton (1980) observed that in a substantial subset of his sample the twins appeared to have divided the parents as primary objects of attachment.[1] Lytton suggested that this may be due, in part, to the tremendous pressures and demands that twins bring to bear on the parents. As a result, each parent may single out a twin as one's own as a way of lowering the overall level of demands that the twinship constitutes. Others have noted similar characteristics in parent-twin relationships (e.g., Burlingham, 1952; Joseph, 1961; Joseph & Tabor, 1961). Many of the subjects in this study similarly indicated a pattern of differential relationship to their parents. There were varying versions of this. In

[1] The concepts of identification and attachment are closely interrelated. Identification is one of the mechanisms through which relations with others become internalized and therefore become part of psychic structure (see Meissner, 1981). In the present context, what is being described as an identification is the presence of psychological features of a parent, for example, which are also found in the personality organization of a twin. Presumably these parental characteristics have become the twin's by virtue of the process of identification. Individuals to whom a child becomes attached, in the sense of having a strong emotional bond with them, also become candidates for identification. That is, the child will attempt to incorporate aspects of these important individuals into his or her own character structure. In the discussion that follows, the term *identification* is used in this sense. It should be kept in mind that children do not draw solely upon secure, positively charged relationships as sources for their identifications. Anna Freud (1936) has illustrated that children can similarly draw upon feared or ambivalently loved objects as sources of identification, as in the classic "identification with the aggressor."

some twinships each twin appeared to be primarily identified with one or the other parent, as was true with the subgroup in Lytton's study. In other twinships, it was not clearly evident that *both* parents were involved in the process. Rather, there appeared to be major differences in the nature and quality of the twins' relationship to the mother, with one twin clearly closer to her, the other less so. Further, in these cases, the twin who did not appear to have the closer relationship to the mother did not necessarily have a closer relationship to the father.

The reasons for such differential attachments are varied. In some instances differential identifications and attachments appeared to be minimally related to the actual characteristics of the twins themselves. For example, in one twinship each parent chose one of the twins' names prenatally. Subsequently, the father became closer to the twin whose name he had selected, while the mother grew closer to the twin whose name she had selected. In several cases, the fathers appear to have chosen the more robust of the twins, while the mothers chose the weaker twin, such as the twin who had spent extra time in the hospital because of prematurity or the twin who had become ill during infancy. With fraternal twins, differential twin-parent relationships may be determined by physical similarities between a twin and one of the parents or by the sex of the twins.

Such differential attachments and subsequent identifications may include subtle psychological factors which are not easily detected. For example, Escalona (1963) describes the mutual accommodation between mother and infant which is necessary in order to optimize development. At play are different aspects of temperament and constitution. In twinships where there are differences in activity level, for example, one mother may wittingly or unwittingly feel more comfortable with her active twin, while another feels more comfortable with the less active twin. Such differences may lay the groundwork for long-term differences in the mother-twin relationship. Similarly, other subtle but powerful factors can be at work in structuring parent-twin relationships. These include a parent's own history of being parented which may directly affect the characteristics of the parenting style. Such differential parenting styles may be more effective with one of the twins than with the other. For example, a less active twin may actually respond better to a parent whose parenting style includes considerable stimulation than will a child who generates considerable self-stimulation to begin with. It is likely that with the latter child, the parent-twin "fit" would be less optimal. Over time, these differences in mutual adaptation would be likely to result in different parent-twin relationships, with concomitant differences between the twins stemming from these identifications.

Many twins provided examples of differential relationships to their parents. In the twinship of Henri and Ian, the twins' mother was French-American and their father was Irish-American. These differences appeared to have played themselves out during the twins' development, with Henri referring to himself as "the French twin," Ian as "the Irish twin." In his interviews, Henri suggested that his mother may have been somewhat closer to him than she was to Ian. He offered as evidence the fact that over the years she had visited him more often.

Jean and Sandie provide another striking example, which has been discussed in some detail in previous chapters. Here again, Sandie was more closely identified with the twins' mother, Jean with their father. These differential identifications appear to have had clear implications in a number of areas of the twins' activities, ranging from childhood play—where Jean played with neighborhood boys, was the tomboy, and went with her father to play golf, whereas Sandie played dolls with the girls next door—to differences in academic and vocational interests—where Jean took math and science courses and went to graduate school in a scientific field, whereas Sandie was decidedly more aesthetically oriented, taking liberal arts courses in college.

Charles and Frank represent a third illustration of differential identification with each of the twins' parents. Charles, a homosexual, was markedly effeminate in his demeanor. Clearly, he was more identified with his mother. Further evidence was to be found in his domestic inclinations, such as his interest in cooking. With these twins, as was true for Henri and Ian, naming appears to have been important.

For example, Charles noted: "My mother's maiden name is my middle name, and so I kind of think that I have a lot of traits from her. I have a lot of feminine traits from my mom, and I am glad I have them, because she had no brothers and sisters, and that line of the family I liked a lot."

Similarly, the following excerpt underscores the strength of the identification between Charles and his mother:

"I tended to go toward music, and mother let me do as much as I wanted to because mother had been active in music when she was younger and enjoyed it thoroughly. This was *her* chance. She would make sure I would practice, and if there was something I didn't understand, she would come in and play it for me so I could hear it. We got to be close on that basis, and Frank never really had piano at all. I enjoyed playing lots of the old stuff . . . when I would play them mom would come in and [she] really enjoyed me playing that. She would say, 'I played that when I was in high school.' It would bring back memories for her. I think we got close on things like that."

On the other hand, Frank clearly identified with his father. Unlike Charles, who dressed in expensive clothes and paid great attention to detail in his dress, Frank generally wore blue jeans, flannel shirts, and boots. Charles described Frank's relationship to his father:

"Frank spent a lot of time [with] and he's sort of like dad. Dad . . . worked on cars between college and [job] and worked as a mechanic for a year. So Dad did a lot of things that were 'macho' things, and he can see himself in Frank, which I'm glad [that] my father has someone to look into [*sic*], because I think parents should [get] to have their genes prolonged like that."

Similarly, during another interview Charles noted: "My grandparents liked Frank better because he's a lot like my father, so it reminded my grandmother of her son, my father, who was her favorite child. It always had been known that that's the way it was, because Frank had this mean streak in him. [Father's mother] was a very hard person, she was a lot like my father, and a lot like my twin brother."

Thus it is clear that in this twinship, major differences between the twins appeared to be consciously related to different relationships with each parent.

Margerie and Melanie provided a somewhat different example with regard to the sources of such differential relationships to their parents. In talking about how the twins' parents tried to treat them as individuals, Margerie described a pattern of interaction in which her mother confided in Margerie in ways that seemed special:

"My sister and one of my brothers are having some conflicts right now because she [Melanie] doesn't think we're all getting equal treatment, and it makes my mother feel terrible. She calls me and tells me that she's doing something for [brother] that she may never have done for any of the rest of us. And she always asks me not to tell Melanie, because she doesn't want Melanie to feel as if she's not getting equal treatment."

During a later interview Margerie returned to this point: "I think now my mother feels closer to me than to Melanie, although she feels close to Melanie in other ways that she can't be close with me—like the fact that they're both mothers now, and they can share a lot of feelings about motherhood [goes on to describe fact that Melanie has a family]. But, I think she [mother] talks to me a whole lot more about her relationship with everyone else in the family, and our relationship, than she does with Melanie."

These excerpts reflect Margerie's sense that her mother treats her somewhat differently than she does Melanie. Other interview material tended to support this view and provided some indications as to possible sources for these differences. For example, in this twinship there were differences in the relative dominance in their relationship; specifically, Melanie tended to be dominant over Margerie when the twins were growing up. During one of her interviews, Margerie had said that "Melanie was probably the more dominant of the two, and she not only tried to boss me around, but she tried to boss my brothers around."

Later in that same interview Margerie noted that her mother, too, was a twin: "Since my mother was a twin, she knew that there was the potential there for me to be plowed under, literally . . . so she had to make the decision, she and daddy, whether it would be best to stick up for me all the time and not let Melanie dominate or let me do it myself."

Interestingly, the twins' mother herself had been dominated by her twin sister when she was growing up:

Margerie: "She [mother] told many stories about how her twin used her and manipulated her and dominated her. She was usually the victim of all the games, and in general she was the one that didn't make the decisions between the two of them."

Perhaps, then, differences in Margerie's and Melanie's relationship to their mother are partly based on differences in the twin's relationship with each other. These differences may have facilitated a differential identification on the part of the twins' mother. Clearly, the mother's position within her own twinship closely paralleled Margerie's relationship with Melanie: both had been dominated in their respective twinships. There is an additional factor as well. In this fraternal twinship, Margerie appears to have resembled her mother physically more than Melanie: "All my life people have said, 'Gee, you look just like your mother.'" The greater physical similarity between Margerie and her mother, together with Margerie's psychological position of being dominated within the twinship, can be understood as contributing to the noted differences in the twins' relationship to their mother.

Further, there are some indications that Melanie actually had a closer identification with the twins' father. For example, Margerie noted that Melanie had some of the father's attributes such as his "academic sort of skills. Like he always used a slide rule as an engineer, that was one of his tools of the trade, and she [Melanie] got in this slide rule competition in junior high and high school and was always really interested in that. Melanie took a lot of advanced math courses."

In other twinships the actual sources of different parent-twin relationships were not always evident, although the twins manifested characteristics which were similar to those just described. As an example of this, Vickie reported:

"A lot of people say I am liked my dad because he was so easy going, and a lot of people say Valery is more like my mom. . . . I think I am like my mom in a lot of ways, and I think I am like my dad in a lot of ways, but if I had to choose, I guess I would say my dad, because I have just learned to be more calm at things. Mom gets real nervous at times and lets things bother her easily. I guess Valery, in a way, tends to be that way sometimes."

Later Vickie added: "At one time I thought mom liked Valery more, that she favored Valery more than me. But I'm sure that everybody goes through that at one time or another—that they're like the black sheep or something."

Interviewer: "When was that?"

Vickie: "I remember it was sometime in the sixth grade. I just remember I used to think, 'Oh, you like Valery more.' I guess I was getting fussed at a lot, but it was just mom that I thought was favoring her."

Finally, Darla provided another example in which there appeared to be early factors at work serving to differentiate the twins in terms of their relationship to their mother and hence to one another. The twins' mother selected Marla's name from a close family member, while naming Darla after someone less personally associated with the family. Darla noted the following with reference to the naming of the twins: "My mother's sister's name is Marla, there was someone in [mother's] class named Darla, and I think she liked the name Marla and was looking for something to kind of go along with that—that's the way I understand it [how the twins' mother selected their names]."

No doubt other factors were also at play, but in this twinship, like the others that have been discussed, there were significant differences between Darla and Marla in terms of the strength of their respective identifications with their mother. For example, the twins' mother was a school teacher, a vocation which might have contributed to her children's own performance in school settings. In fact, Marla had a much more successful academic history than did Darla. Furthermore, Marla's advanced degree was directly related to mother's career (it involved work within school settings), while Darla's career was in a field that her mother had always "looked down on."

This particular twinship illustrates that each twin does not always get "his own parent." While Marla seemed to have the stronger identification with her mother, Darla could hardly boast of a parallel relationship with her father, as suggested by the following comment: "I was always daddy's little girl. We didn't do a lot of things with him [though]. Daddy would have done better if mother had had a boy."

One important source of differentiation for twins is their differing relationships with their parents. Although it is not necessarily a factor in all twinships, many of the twins participating in this study exhibited at least some degree of major differential identification with their parents or else major differences in their relationship to their mothers, which formed the basis for significant differences between the twins themselves. In the following section, the role of competition in the twinship is examined.

Competition

Competition and rivalry, while varying in intensity, are ubiquitous phenomena between siblings (e.g., A. Freud, 1965; Legg, Sherick, & Wadland, 1974). Numerous authors have observed that, for twins, competition tends to be heightened (e.g., Burlingham, 1946, 1952; Karpman, 1953; Joseph, 1961; Joseph & Tabor, 1961). Most often the sources of this heightened competition are linked to competition for parental attention, expecially from the mother (e.g., Lytton, 1980). Lytton's work documented empirically that each twin partici-pates in less individual interaction with adults than does the single-ton. That twins must vie for attention is not surprising in this con-text, for there are simply fewer resources to go around. Much of the material derived from the subjects who participated in this study tended to corroborate this conceptualization; however, an equally important relationship became evident between competition and the emergence of differences between twins.

For many of the twins in the present study, competition seemed to be an important concern. The wish to avoid competing with one another was often quite marked. But their descriptions also made it evident that in many life situations competition is inescapable. Jean's observation illustrates this clearly in the context of school:

"We didn't like to compete, because it felt really uncomfortable. When I had to compete against Sandie, I just tried to make it seem like Sandie was just like any other person. Even at the end of high school . . . when they had the award presentations, I sort of felt funny when I got the National Merit Scholarship and she didn't. That was sort of a big thing, the biggest thing that happened in high school pretty much. PSAT's are not broken down into subjects, really. So I think I sort of felt funny when I did a lot better than her. When people would ask, 'How did you guys do?' we tried not to talk about it too much."

Interviewer: "Can you tell me what that feeling was like?"

Jean: "It feels bad because you don't really want to do it to yourself, but you are forced into situations where sometimes. . . . We care about each other, and we feel badly about being hurt—or maybe if you would have done something different, but yet you don't want to cheat yourself either, so . . ."

Interviewer: "So you were telling me what that felt like."

Jean: "I felt—it just sort of created a little boundary that you didn't want to create, an awkward situation. It's like I never liked to talk about tests after the test, and I've always felt funny about people you come up to and [who] say, 'How did you do?' It's even worse when it's your sister, and you don't want to say something that will discourage her, or you don't want to hear something that will discourage you."

Jean's description made very clear the difficulties engendered by competitive situations. There is a sense that to succeed must be at the expense of one's twin, yet not to do well may be a loss to oneself, neither alternative being a very comfortable one. In this instance, competition also creates a not-altogether-desired boundary between the twins. Although Jean's illustration makes reference specifically to school, other situations that create a competitive atmosphere between twins are not difficult to imagine.

For example, Vickie stated the following in reference to participating on the same swimming team: "We don't really like to compete against each other. I just don't. But in a way, it just made me work harder in other stuff—not necessarily to outbeat her, but just to be good. We have had to swim competitively together, and I usually win, only because . . . there was one summer that I worked out a lot more than she did, and I just really got ahead of her."

As the examples illustrate, competition between twins can create difficulties for them. In particular, the choice between undermining one's own potential or having to endure the discomfort of achieving more than one's twin is a painful dilemma and one that is difficult to resolve. For many of the twins, however, being different from each other helped the twins avoid these painful emotions. In this sense competition can be considered as a source of differentiation. Commonly, carving out different interests or areas of expertise was described as a means of avoiding competing directly with one another. In the following excerpts, for example, differentiation is described as a means of avoiding competition:

Sandie: "We had different majors [in college], so that worked out real well for us, because a lot of competition was forced upon us. People compare you, so having different interests spared us a little."

Dianne: "Our life-styles are totally different. In a way it is real good because it takes us out of the competitive rink. We are just not like each other—we can have different standards."

Martha: "He's [twin brother] probably one of the greatest people I know. I really like him. I think that the fact that we were of different sexes alleviated a lot of competition between us: I didn't play football, and he didn't play majorette! So we kind of developed into our own person [*sic*], yet never really let go of the tie that was between us."

Melanie: "In high school we were involved in different activities. We could allow each other to go off and really excel in this area without having to be right in there too, in competing for [student government] office or whatever."

This approach to resolving the problem of competition has a number of drawbacks. The most important of these is the ambiguity which such a solution creates regarding identity, as Jean illustrates:

"I think also, we were both trying to be different a lot too, and that might have had influences. Like we tried to get involved in different activities, and I was sort of going over to math and science, and she was sort of going over to the English and history end of the academic scene. How much was because we really wanted to go that way, and how much was because we wanted to be different persons from each other and be our own persons? I think the push from my family might have been not conscious. They really are achievement oriented . . . [this way] we would each have our own thing that we could excel in, and so that way we wouldn't be compared as much. I think it took a lot of pressure off of us."

In other words, differentiation, as a means of alleviating the difficult emotions involved in competing openly with one's twin can create other problems, such as, in this instance, raising questions about the authenticity of the choices one makes regarding areas of interest and involvement.

These excerpts suggest that differentiation is fostered by a wish to avoid competition and its painful emotional implications. While the material makes this evident, the relationship between competition and differentiation is considerably more complex. Other material from these same subjects suggests that delineating areas of differentiation from one another not only functions as a mechanism for avoiding competition between twins, it can also have the opposite effect. For example, in some instances differences between the twins, real or imagined, major or subtle, subsequently created arenas for competition between them.

The relationship between competition and differentiation is illustrated in terms of physical differences between a pair of identical twins. These subtle differences were somewhat exaggerated by Vickie, thereby becoming a source of competition.

Vickie and Valery were both attractive identical twins. This had been documented objectively for them through a variety of beauty contests.

Vickie: "At one time I felt that Valery was a lot prettier than I and used to tell people, 'Oh, she is prettier than I: that's how you can tell us apart.' And I am not saying now, 'I think I am prettier than her,' I think that we just have different looks. I think her smile is different from mine, mine goes straight and hers curls up. I think her nose is different from mine; there are some features that I like about her and some features that I like about me and vice versa. I used to tell Valery that I thought she was prettier than I was, and she would say that we looked alike."

Vickie said these feelings were altered somewhat in her senior year of high school when she ran for beauty queen at her school: "[Valery] didn't run for it, and I got something like third runner-up. For a while, I thought she was prettier and almost thought, 'What's wrong with me?' It made me feel a lot better that I got third runner-up—at least I didn't feel like I was ugly. So, now I think we both look a lot alike. . . . Valery was real happy for me and she was saying, 'Boy, if I had gotten in it, I would have won.' But she was just kidding. But she had her chance, and she really didn't want to wear a bathing suit, because at that time I was a little skinnier than her. I still am, because I am taller—it makes a difference. It made me feel good, too, when she said, 'If my figure was like yours, I would run [in the same contest].' I think it runs through her mind every now and then—if she had run, what would have happened?"

Earlier the same year of high school both twins had been selected to run for a different contest—the school's homecoming queen competition ("They choose you—you don't really enter").

Interviewer: "What was the outcome of that?"

Vickie: "[Friend] won it, Valery got first runner-up, and I got second runner-up. Then in the middle of the year they chose class favorites, and she [Valery] won it. I wanted her to make it, I didn't care if I made it . . . it didn't really bother me, but it did a little bit. But I, to me, I had already won what I wanted to win [the earlier mentioned beauty contest]. But I don't know what the feeling was that I felt, but I felt a little something when she got first runner-up and I got second runner-up. But then I thought, 'Hey, it's no big deal, it was probably only by a few points anyway.' Even if it wasn't—it was no big deal."

Debbie and Dianne demonstrated the intimate connection between competition and differentiation as well. As with Vickie and Valery, the presence of certain differences between them became focal points for competition in their relationship.

Interviewer: "Were you compared by your parents?"

Dianne: "Constantly we were compared, we still are."

Interviewer: "What kinds of comparisons?"

Dianne: "Report cards."

Debbie: "Yes. At the end of the semester, report cards would be held up, 'Okay, you did better than you, who was smarter, who was this, who was that . . .'"

Dianne: "Smarter or stronger."

Debbie: "The main issue in our family was intelligence. Dianne was the smarter one, and I was the stronger one."

Later in this same interview, Debbie and Dianne elaborated on this theme:

Debbie: "Dianne, in my mind, was in a better position because she was considered the smarter one. I was stronger, but yet dumber, so that was the implication that I've always had."

Dianne: "Except that you were more popular though . . . we were extremely competitive. We internalized all the comparison-doing ourselves, and we did it to each other constantly."

This description reflects other elements of how competition functions in this twinship and how it relates to differentiation. The characteristics that form points of differentiation (whether actual or created) in intelligence, strength, and sociability also constitute points of tension. Rather than resolving possible concerns regarding identity integration, the twins generate considerable ambivalence by the sense that certain capacities or characteristics have been distributed unequally. Dianne envies Debbie's popularity, while Debbie envies Dianne's intellectual performance. This sense of unequally distributed characteristics only exacerbates the feeling that one has lost something important. Recognition or demarcation of certain abilities or talents feels like a taking away. The differentiating elements which might serve to avoid competition may actually contribute to increased competitive feelings, especially if those differentiating elements involve praise, acknowledgment, or other rewards.

Margerie illustrates the theme that activities, interests, or behavior, which result in differences between the twins and hence in differential acknowledgment, can be problematic. In this instance there seems to be a feeling that the recognition of differences is experienced as a loss to oneself or at one's expense when one's twin is being acknowledged.

Margerie: "I felt that they [parents] recognized that each twin had different personalities that needed to be handled differently. [They] tried to treat [us] as individuals. [But] I felt that they encouraged Melanie in things because they recognized certain abilities in her and sometimes didn't recognize that I had other abilities that were just as worthwhile. But I never felt that they thought that she was the best twin."

Other twins described similar feelings.

Sandie: "I have always been interested in literature and art, and I did better in that than [Jean] did, whereas Jean has always been attracted to math and science. In elementary school her flair for math and science was already established, whereas other things—I don't know, if they took more time to show themselves or whatever, you never comment on a third grader's facility with language."

Regarding others' comparisons of the twins, Sandie added: "I would say, 'I have other things that I am interested in, that I do OK in, so you can leave me alone.' It still comes through [in the present] with people who don't understand, who are insensitive."

It should be remembered that these descriptions may not accurately reflect whatever actual differences were present in the way the twins were treated. For example, in some twinships each twin felt that the other was recognized in ways that felt somewhat unfair. The accounts merely reflect differences in *perception*. Of course, perceptions are important and substantive in psychological functioning, since they can influence behavior, emotion, and other perceptions profoundly. In twinship, that each twin might have different areas of talent that are reinforced or acknowledged by the parents does not necessarily mitigate the feeling that the other is favored or that the other's characteristics are the preferred ones to have.

Feelings that one twin is doing well at the expense of the other twin are fostered by fantasies such as one represented by Darla: "Marla said on the phone that sometimes she felt like there was only a certain amount of happiness, and that when one of us had it, the other just didn't. It was like we both couldn't be happy at the same time." Such feelings can clearly accentuate the competitive feelings within the twinship. These feelings are closely related to common conceptualizations of the sources of competition in twinship.

Darla provided a similar example in another interview: "I think maybe there was a difference in college when Marla was very political and did all of these . . . things that she became very well known for, like became student body secretary and was queen for a fraternity, and a lot of things. I guess I had some things, but I never felt quite equal. I feel at times when Marla is down that I really want to help her, and I'd probably do anything to help her. At times when Marla is really high and doing real well and I have to be around her and I'm not doing so hot for some reason, then I feel a little resentful. It's like I'm preparing myself and then I'll want to move away, want to be away in order to regain whatever it is that I have for myself."

This material emphasizes the close connection between differentiation and competition. As is often noted in the clinical literature pertaining to twins, cometition is a common feature of twin relationships. In some instances, differentiation between twins seems to circumvent the competitive feelings which appear to be inherent in the twin situation. This is the case because having different characteristics, interests, or involvements creates separate areas of functioning that are mutually understood by each twin as belonging to the other. It is as if within these defined areas a twin is free to develop and excel without fear that such achievement may be at the co-twin's expense.

A study by Schachter, Shore, Feldman-Rotman, Marquis, & Campbell (1976) supports this interpretation. These researchers examined two- and three-child families for the extent to which (non-twin) children perceived themselves to be similar or dissimilar (de-identification) to their siblings. They found that for the first pair of siblings in three-child families the extent of de-identification was significantly higher for same-sex siblings than was the case for opposite-sex siblings. In another study Schachter, Gilutz, Shore, & Adler (1978) found de-identification to be highest for the first two siblings, followed by the second and third siblings, with comparisons between the first and third siblings showing the lowest percentage of de-identification. Schachter et al. (1978) concluded that their results were compatible with a rivalry-defense hypothesis for de-identification—that is, de-identification is fostered by an attempt to diminish rivalry between siblings. This is precisely the view being suggested here. As the twin subjects in the present study illustrate, competition within the twinship can be distressing and painful. In this sense the feelings associated with competition foster differentiation, since there is considerable motivation to avoid them. In other circumstances, however, areas of differentiation appeared to fuel competitive feelings. A key factor may be the relationship between the specific dimensions upon which twins differ and the values and interests which exist within a particular family.

More important may be the felt sense that emotional supplies are not available, resulting in a readiness to perceive parental responses to one's twin as a depletion of one's own potential sources of support and comfort or as a reflection of treatment which is preferential, when this is not necessarily the case. Under the sway of such feelings, differentiation may foster competitive feelings toward one's twin rather than dampen them. Thus, there seems to be a circular or interactive relationship between competition and differentiation wherein competition fuels differentiation, which in turn fuels competition. Nevertheless, the wish to avoid competition appears to be an important motivating force which fosters differentiation between twins.

In this chapter two important sources of differentiation in twinship have been examined: twins' differential identifications with their parents, and the role of competition within their relationship. Clearly, many potential sources for particular differences exist between individuals. An infinite number of life experiences are possible which contribute substantially to an individual's sense of oneself, to the talents that an individual develops, or to the ways in which an individual attempts to express personal uniqueness. Further, for twins who are not monozygotic, as for nontwins, genetic factors may also contribute in important ways to differentiation depending on the traits under consideration. In these examples, however, the contribution of two environmental factors to the differentiation of characteristics within the twinship was illustrated. Differential identification with parents has been discussed in the twin literature as an important feature of some twinships (e.g., Burlingham, 1952; Joseph, 1961; Joseph & Tabor, 1961; Lytton, 1980). In this chapter we have seen the manner in which such relationships contribute to a twin's definition of self. Similarly, competition is a frequently noted characteristic of twin relationships, although it is less often thought of as a source of motivation for twins to differentiate.

These two examples of ways in which twins become different from one another are informative; however, a more central consideration is that differentiation, whatever its source, appears to be an important issue for twins. Twins frequently *want* to be different from one another, and others often use differentiation as a yardstick with which to assess the twins' so-called normality. The examples offered in this chapter underscore the complexity of such an issue from the standpoint of a twin's subjective experience, while simultaneously suggesting that the twin situation, including the unusual circumstances that it creates in terms of parent-child relationships, contributes to the forces of differentiation.

7

Survey of Mothers of Twins

An early phase of this project involved a survey of mothers of twins in which they were asked about their perspectives on a number of twin issues. This was an effort to gather descriptive data on the early development of twins. These mothers were not related to the twins that were interviewed. This effort was to gather information rather than to test hypotheses.

The questionnaire that was administered to mothers of twins covered four general areas: demographics, the mother's pregnancy and the twins' neonatal period and infancy, more general psychological issues for twins and the mothers' perceptions of these, and the mothers' experiences of parenting twins (the questionnaire can be found in appendix B). In keeping with the approach taken in the interviews with twins, the questionnaire was devised primarily as a vehicle for asking the mothers open-ended questions, rather than asking structured questions or administering rating scales. The specific topics covered were those which seemed a priori to be important, although these were also based on previous reports in the literature. Once the questionnaire had been constructed, it was disseminated through the Texas organization of Mothers of Multiples, and 130 questionnaires were returned.

Numerous researchers have used semistructured interview formats to gather data about twinship (e.g., Brown et al., 1967; Wilson et al., 1971; Torgersen & Kringlen, 1978). Although not administered via interviews, in many respects the present format was similar to these efforts. It should be noted that mothers have been found to be reliable reporters of their children's early developmental experiences (e.g., Costello, 1975; Koch, 1966). For example, Koch was able to check mothers' retrospective reports of birth weights in her study and found that a "mother's reports of her twins' birth weight agreed well with the hospital record" (p. 1270).

The questionnaire contained two kinds of questions: those for which specific, readily codable responses were required (such as demographics) and those for which the respondents gave open-ended, unstructured answers. The former were copied directly from the questionnaires onto data sheets. For the open-ended questions, a different procedure was followed. A coding grid was developed to score the mothers' responses on each of these questions. Subsequently, raters who were blind to the zygosity of the twins coded the open-ended questions. To prevent raters' preconceptions about twins from influencing their ratings, the following steps were taken: The mothers' responses for each question were transcribed and assigned a number. Because twins sometimes had names that rhymed, their names were deleted from these transcripts and replaced by "A" or "B." Raters then coded the responses question by question, rather than questionnaire by questionnaire, to protect against possible halo effects. Twenty-five percent of all the questions (structured and unstructured) were rated by two raters independently to ascertain interrater reliability. Only questions for which an alpha coefficient of .70 or better was attained are reported here. Unless otherwise noted, the results are from the following distribution of subjects within the three twin groups: identical twins (MZ) = 62, fraternal same-sex twins (DZSS) = 42, fraternal opposite-sex twins (DZOS) = 26.

This sample was predominantly Caucasian and middle-class (e.g., 73% of the mothers and 82% of the fathers had at least some college).

Results

In the present sample, parents tended to be somewhat older at the time they had their twins than would be true for the general population of parents, a finding which is in keeping with others reported in this literature. For example, in the study by Matheny et al. (1981), the average age of the mothers was 26.5 years—virtually identical to the mothers in the present sample.

One-way ANOVA's were performed to see if there was a relationship between the age of the mother or father at the time of the twins' birth

Table 1. Demographic Characteristics of the Twins and Their Parents

	Total	MZ	DZSS	DZOS
Zygosity		48%	32%	20%
Age of twins (months)	34	34	32	38
Sex of twins				
Male	41%	58%	42.5%	50%
Female	38%	42%	57.5%	50%
(DZOS)	21%			
Mother's age at twin birth (average)	27	27	26	
Father's age at twin birth (average)	30	29	29	
History of twins in mother's family	72%	67%	85%	
History of twins in father's family	63%	51%	30%	
Both mother and father have twins in family	48%	38%	27%	

MZ = Monozygotic, identical twins
DZSS = Dizygotic, fraternal same-sex twins
DZOS = Dizygotic, fraternal opposite-sex twins

and the three twin groups. The results were not significant. Chi-square analyses were performed to see whether a history of having twins in the mother's family, father's family, or both families was related to the three twin groups. For mothers, the history data were not significant. For fathers, however, the results were significant at the $p < .03$ level ($\chi^2 = 6.98$, $df = 2$). The low incidence of DZOS twins who had fathers with a history of twins in the family appears to account for this finding, since 85 percent of the DZOS twins had mothers with a history of twins in their families, while only 30 percent of the DZOS twins had fathers with a similar history. The tendency as seen in Table 1 is for mother's history of twins to figure more prominently across twinship groups. This is especially true for DZOS twins.

The present sample is not representative of twinships as a whole. The subjects are drawn from mothers who are members of an organization that has monthly meetings and, in many ways, functions as a support group for mothers of twins. Further, a considerable amount of information about twinship is disseminated through these clubs. Thus, membership in a Mothers of Multiples club may well shape the perceptions and attitudes of these mothers in ways that make them different from other mothers of twins. It may also be that a particular group of mothers has self-selected into these organizations. Major discrepancies between the data derived from this study and other reports in the literature might be one indication of systematic bias in the sample. But, for the most part, such discrepancies have not been found.

The distribution of twinships in this sample is not representative. Theoretically, one would expect each of the three twinship groups (MZ, DZSS, DZOS) to be equally represented (Loehlin & Nichols, 1976); however, the higher rate of infant mortality for MZ twins and male children would result in an expected frequency of MZ twins which was somewhat lower for the general twin population. Instead, in this sample MZ's are the largest group. Many studies have similar overrepresentation of MZ twins (e.g., Buss et al., 1973; Dworkin, 1979; Loehlin & Nichols, 1976; Torgersen and Kringlen, 1978). Thus, generalizations to the entire population of twins must be handled with care.

Chi-square analyses relating necessity of extra time in the hospital, length of that extra stay, prematurity, and pregnancy (and labor) complications to the three twin groups were not significant. However, analyses revealed trends in the direction of decreased likelihood of prematurity for DZSS twins ($\chi^2 = 4.59$, $df = 2$, $p < .10$) and an increased likelihood of pregnancy complications for DZOS twins ($\chi^2 = 4.75$, $df = 2$, $p < .09$).

One-way ANOVA's were performed to test for possible relationships between the attainment of developmental milestones and a number of variables relating to the early twin situation. ANOVA's relating developmental milestones to complications in pregnancy, medical problems in infancy, and birth weight were not significant. Although there were no significant differences among the three twin groups in terms of when they began to crawl, there was a very weak trend ($p < .13$) for DZOS twins to begin walking somewhat earlier than either MZ or DZSS twins. Further, prematurity appeared to slow the attainment of the developmental milestones: crawling (strong trend, $p < .07$), walking ($p < .05$).

Analyses were performed to see whether there were significant within-pair differences in weight across twin groups. Two-tailed *t*-tests comparing within-pair differences revealed the differences between the heavier and lighter twins to be highly significant across twinship groups (MZ $t = 7.09$, $p < .0001$; DZSS $t = 8.46$, $p < .0001$; DZOS $t = 2.99$, $p < .006$).

These analyses were also performed to check for sex differences. No sex differences were found for most of the variables in this study. This is in keeping with Wilson et al. (1971), who found few sex differences in their sample of twins across a wide range of variables.

As is evident from Table 2, the present sample shows that twin births constitute an at-risk situation. Almost two-thirds of the mothers reported complications during pregnancy and delivery (e.g., high blood pressure, toxemia, and breech birth). Further, approximately half of the babies were reported to be premature, and the average weight for the entire sample (87 ounces) is low. More than a third of the twins had to spend extra time in the hospital postnatally ($M = 3.2$ weeks). Finally, approximately a quarter of the twins had a major illness during infancy. Together, these statistics indicate graphically that twins must, on average, overcome an unusual number of concrete developmental obstacles early in life.

Of the variables just noted, prematurity and low birth weight have been the most studied. These two categories are actually somewhat overlapping, since prematurity is often defined in terms of birth weight, with infants weighing less than 88 ounces considered premature (Barden, 1983; Koch, 1966; Mittler, 1971).[1] At 87 ounces, the mean birth weight for this sample is below the gauge for prematurity defined by birth weight. The incidence of prematurity defined by gestational age (37 weeks gestation or less) is unknown in the present sample. It is not clear whether mothers were using gestational age criteria or birth weight criteria in answering this question. According to Sweet (1973), of the infants in his study who weighed less

[1] The literature is inconsistent in how weight figures are reported. Depending on the author, 2,500 grams, 5 ½ pounds, or 88 ounces is used as the point of reference. Obviously, all reflect the same actual weight. For purposes of consistency, the present sample and comparisons with other samples are discussed in terms of ounces.

148

Table 2. *Neonatal Period and Infancy*

	Total	MZ	DZSS	DZOS
Complications in pregnancy	64%	63%	55%	81%
Twins were premature	47%	51%	31%	52%
Mean weight at birth (ounces)	87	87	88	84
SD (ounces)	21	21	23	19
Mean within-pair differences (ounces)		8.3	10.1	11.5
Extra time in hospital (at least one twin)	36%	49%	36%	35%
Length of extra stay in hospital	3.2	3.1	3.0	3.8
SD (in weeks)	2.3	2.4	1.9	2.9
Major medical problems (first year)	27%	28%	24%	27%
One of the twins	11%	10%	17%	4%
Both of the twins	16%	18%	7%	23%
Developmental milestones				
Mean age first twin to crawl (weeks)		29	29	28
Mean age second twin to crawl		32	32	34
Mean age first twin to walk (weeks)		49	48	44
Mean age second twin to walk		51	52	52

than 88 ounces, approximately two-thirds were not full-term at birth.

This sample actually has a somewhat lower incidence of prematurity than that reported by Koch (1966), who found that 56 percent of her sample of twins were premature (defined by birth weight), and is in keeping with Field, Walden, Widmayer, & Breenbery (1975), who reported an incidence of prematurity (defined by gestational age) of 46 percent. In the general population, the incidence of low birth weight is approximately 7.5 percent (Barden, 1983). This figure has remained fairly stable during the last decade. One can readily see that the likelihood of being born premature is many times higher for twins than for the general population. As reported by other researchers (e.g., Brown et al., 1967; Koch, 1966), there was no significant relationship between prematurity and zygosity in the present sample.

The potential complications associated with prematurity are many. Sweet (1973) cites neonatal asphyxia, hypoglycemia, thermal regulation problems, and polycythemia as common problems in preterm infants. Studies relating prematurity to subsequent developmental interference have been ambiguous in their results. Cohen and Beckwith (1979) found preterm infants to be functioning within the normal range on a series of developmental tests (Gesell, Bayley, sensorimotor, receptive language). On the other hand, Koch (1966) found trends in the opposite direction. Looking at older twin children, Koch found "a disposition for those of early birth . . . to perform less well than term children in ability tests and in major school subjects" (p. 1277).

A number of studies have reported premature infants to be at risk in terms of socioemotional development (e.g., Fraiberg, 1980; Klaus & Kennel, 1973; Sugar, 1982). Among the sources for these difficulties are reported problems in infant-parent attachment. Difficulties in attachment may be fostered initially by the separation and lack of contact produced by prolonged hospitalization (Klaus & Kennel, 1973). In addition, once home, premature infants often receive less adequate stimulation from their mothers (Sugar, 1982). Further complicating the development of attachment between infant and mother is the mother's reaction to delivering a premature infant. Kaplan and Mason (1960) concluded that these reactions often represent an "acute emotional crisis."

Other evidence supports the view that prematurity may affect parent-twin relationships. For example, Field et al. (1975) found that, in twinships where there were differences of at least 15 percent of the twins' weights, mothers differed in their perceptions of each of the twins in infancy. The smaller twin was described as smiling more, more inclined to "seek love," and "more accepting of people," while also demanding more attention and being more prone to temper tantrums, crying, and feeding and sleeping problems (all significant at the $p < .05$ level). These differences persisted when mothers and twins were reassessed at one year. Field et al. (1975) found evidence that mothers were providing "compensatory treatment" to the twin with lower birth weight, since mothers continued to see the smaller child as more loving and accepting, for example, but also because they behaved differently with them in play. Similar compensatory behavior for infants of lower weight has been reported by others as well (Allen, Pollin, & Hoffer, 1971; Allen et al., 1976; Gifford, Muraski, Brazelton, & Young, 1966). Weight differences between twins have also been linked to other variables. For example, Koch (1966) and Tienari (1963) both found that birth weight was related to physical and psychological dominance by the heavier twin over the co-twin.

Thirty-eight percent of the twins in the present study had to spend additional time in the hospital neonatally, and over a quarter of the sample had at least one twin with major medical problems during the first year of life. The literature contains similar findings (e.g., Barr & Stevenson, 1961). Although involving a small number of subjects, Cohen et al. (1972) examined ten twins longitudinally with in-depth observations using different assessment techniques. They started with prenatal interviews and had detailed information for the twins' early development, including data on the twins' deliveries. They developed the First-Week Evaluation Scale (FES), which included as variables the following dimensions: health, physiological adaptation, calmness, vigor, attention, and neurology. The following groups tended to have higher (more optimal) FES scores: female infants, firstborn infants, infants who had a higher birth weight, and those infants who were "vertex deliveries." When assessed several years later (in nursery school), the high FES children contrasted sharply with the low FES children. High FES children talked more and coped better, while low FES children were more dependent on their mothers and more fearful of strangers. These differences were either statistically significant or reflected strong trends. Cohen et al. also found that, while all of their twin subjects had a large number of medical problems, this was especially true for low FES children, who had more severe illnesses and had spent more time in the hospital. They concluded that the better endowed the newborn, the more likely that infant was to be secure, trusting, and developmentally advanced during the first year and the more competent that infant was likely to be as a toddler. The small number of subjects in the Cohen et al. study requires that the findings be interpreted with caution. Nevertheless, they underscore the potential impact of early stress on subsequent development. Evidence has increasingly indicated that specific behaviors can be identified early in infancy which persist into later years (Escalona, 1968; Kagan & Moss, 1962; Sroufe & Waters, 1977; Thomas, Birch, Chess, Herzog, & Korn, 1964). Cohen and Beckwith (1979) found social differences in premature infants by one month of age—differences which were highly related to assessments of competence at two years of age. Similarly, looking at twins, Matheny et al. (1981) have demonstrated the continuity of behavioral patterns once these become established during infancy. Studies indicating continuity of personality organization, as well as those linking twinship with a higher incidence of early experiences which are potentially deleterious for socioemotional development, underscore the likelihood that twins are at greater risk than nontwins for developmental interference.

The reports of developmental milestones reflect some interesting differences among the three twin groups. Though not statistically significant, there is a tendency for MZ twins to be closest to one another in the attainment of crawling and walking, while opposite-sex fraternals reflected the biggest discrepancy. This is evident when the time lag between the first and the second twin in the attainment of crawling and walking is compared. For example, the mean difference for crawling between MZ, DZSS, and DZOS twins, respectively, was as follows: 2.6 (weeks), 3.3, and 6.1. The differences between the first and second twin to walk reflect similar trends: MZ = 2.6 (weeks), DZSS = 3.5, DZOS = 7.1. Since MZ twins are most alike, the extent of intrapair divergence between each of the three twin groups on these two developmental tasks is suggestive of a genetic contribution to the development of motor activity. The same is true for average within-pair differences in weight in that MZ twin differences were the smallest.

The mothers of twins were asked to describe their feeding practices during the twins' first year. The results are reported in table 3. A chi-squared analysis indicated no significant differences between method of feeding and the three main groups.

Given the presumed difficulties involved in breast-feeding two

Table 3. Method of Feeding Twins

	Total	MZ	DZSS	DZOS
Breast-Feeding	22%	26%	24%	12%
Bottle-Feeding	43%	35%	45%	58%
Both	34%	39%	31%	31%

infants, that nearly a quarter of the MZ and DZSS mothers breast fed exclusively for at least several months during infancy, as shown in table 3, was somewhat surprising. A number of mothers noted that this was actually easier for them. In the context of constant demands by their twin infants, several mothers reported that breast-feeding was actually "time efficient" since it saved them the task of mixing and heating formula, washing bottles, and sterilizing nipples.

This group of mothers identified their husbands and the twins' grandmothers as the major sources of help during the twins' first year of life. Mothers rated the degree of help of various people on a 1 to 5 scale (1 = not involved at all, 5 = very involved). Fathers received an average rating of 4.5 (N = 129); grandmothers 3.7 (N = 125). Twins' older siblings and others received low ratings.

The only significant relationship between extent of support and twinship group was for fathers, who were reported to be significantly more helpful by mothers of MZ twins than was true for mothers of DZSS twins ($\chi^2 = 9.37$, $df = 4$, $p < .05$).

Mothers were asked to respond to the following open-ended questions: (1) What was most rewarding to you when your twins were infants? (2) What was most difficult for you when your twins were infants?

There are few differences between the groups of twins in terms of mothers' reports for most rewarding and most difficult features of parenting twins (see table 4). A series of chi-square analyses found neither the "rewarding" variables nor the "difficult" variables to be significantly related to twinship group. Surprisingly, mothers' assessments of difficulties or rewards in raising their twins were not significantly related to their perceived levels of support or help from others. Similarly, the degree of reported rivalry between the twins was also not related to the "difficult" variables. The one item in both of the

Table 4. Most Rewarding and Most Difficult Features of Parenting Twins

Rewarding	Total	MZ	DZSS	DZOS
Watching them grow up	32%	28%	39%	31%
Feeling needed by the twins	16%	22%	15%	8%
Loving the twins	24%	28%	12%	31%
Other	28%	22%	34%	30%
Difficult				
Caring for both twins at once	67%	66%	64%	77%
Getting housework done	15%	15%	17%	12%
Interfered with career	3%	2%	5%	4%
Other	16%	17%	14%	7%

response groups which was most often noted by mothers of all three twin groups is the difficulty of "caring for both twins at once." Clearly, a great many mothers felt this to be a difficult task. Following are some sample responses for this item:

"No sleep! Constant demands."

"Being tired—the ability to cope with the demands was lessened so much by lack of sleep. No time for myself. The boys were about a year old when I took up jogging early in the morning just to get away and have a half-hour to myself."

"Most difficult thing was finding time for things other than feedings."

"When they would both cry at the same time."

"Most frustrating—trying to keep two fussy babies contented at once."

"When they were both hungry, or anytime they both needed me and cried for me."

"I would feel extremely guilty when I would be feeding one and the other would cry. If I had had a singleton, I would never not have responded to their cry for attention. With twins, I often felt very pulled and inadequate to meet their needs when both needed me at the same time."

"Getting up in the middle of the night—double! You'd get one fed and changed and back to sleep and get yourself back to sleep and thirty minutes later, time to do it again."

154

Table 5. *Twins' Use of Transitional Objects,*
Imaginary Companions, and Private Language

Special Object	Total	MZ	DZSS	DZOS
Twin A	13%	10%	10%	20%
Twin B	11%	8%	10%	16%
Both	36%	38%	41%	28%
Imaginary Companion	9%	13%	3%	8%
Private Language	29%	26%	32%	32%

"I felt I was always feeding babies—never getting a chance to do the things my husband and I wanted to do."

Developmental Phenomena

In a series of questions the mothers in this sample were asked whether either of their twins had a favorite object (other than pacifier) to which the child was especially attached, an imaginary companion, or if the twins shared a private language.

None of the variables was significantly related to type of twin-ship. (N's for imaginary companion were as follows: MZ = 53, DZSS = 31, DZOS = 25; for private language: MZ = 51, DZSS = 31, DZOS = 25.)

The incidence of children using special, or transitional objects is presumably high, since this is understood to be a normal and somewhat universal developmental phenomenon (Winnicott, 1953). In this sample, approximately 60 percent of the twins are reported to have had such special objects. The actual percentage is probably higher than noted in table 5, since some of these subjects were actually too young to have developed such attachments. There appear to be few differences among the three twinship groups in this respect.

According to Svendson (1934), 13 percent of all children have imaginary companions. Nagera (1981) notes that imaginary companions are relatively rare prior to the age of two and a half. Since approximately 42 percent of the present sample was under the age of two, a conservative estimate of the actual incidence of imaginary companions (excluding twins under the age of two who are presumably too young to have developed them) is 16 percent for the total sample. This is still in keeping with the figures reported by Svendsen. Taking this age correction into consideration, the incidence of imaginary companions among the three twin groups would be as follows: MZ = 19 percent; DZSS = 4 percent; DZOS = 13 percent. It is unclear why DZSS twins would have such a lower incidence when compared with the other groups. Nagera notes that imaginary companions may serve a variety of developmental functions for children, depending on the child's particular circumstances. These functions include externalization, mastery of various feelings and conflicts, handling feelings of loneliness, and dealing with the birth of a sibling, among others. The present survey was not sufficiently detailed to assess the nature or content of these imaginary companions. Nagera (1981) and Fraiberg (1959) emphasize that the presence of imaginary companions is a normal developmental event for most children who have them, except in those instances where the child's investment in fantasy interferes significantly with ties to reality.

The mothers' reports of their twins having a private language were somewhat sketchy. Often these seemed to include a limited number of words which the mothers had a difficult time understanding. Further, these manifestations of twins' private language appeared to be transient rather than stable features of twin communication patterns. The incidence of a more elaborated system of communication which was shared exclusively between the twins was much less frequent. Here again, however, the age of this sample makes it difficult to know with certainty how frequent such communication is among twins.

Questions relating to the degree to which twins looked alike were posed. For example, the mothers were asked whether their twins looked alike, whether it was difficult to tell the twins apart (parents might feel that their twins were similar in appearance yet not difficult to tell apart), whether the parents had ever mixed them up, and whether the twins were ever confused as to whom they were.

These results from table 6, not surprisingly, were significant. A series of chi-squared analyses comparing MZ and DZSS twins revealed the following results: Zygosity by *look alike*: $\chi^2 = 32.35$, $df = 1$, $p < .0001$; zygosity by *difficult to tell apart*: $\chi^2 = 34.77$, $df = 3$, $p < .0001$; zygosity by *ever mix them up*: $\chi^2 = 9.00$, $df = 1$, $p < .002$; zygosity by *twins get confused*: $\chi^2 = 2.93$, $df = 1$, $p < .08$.

Table 6. Twins' Physical Similarity

	Total	MZ	DZSS	DZOS
Do the twins look alike?	66%	97%	45%	20%
Are they difficult to tell apart? (mean score where 1 = easy, 4 = very hard)		3.1	1.7	1.0
Have you and your husband ever mixed them up? (yes)	63%	77%	48%	12%
Are the twins ever confused about who they are? (yes)		31%	17%	0

Across a range of questions relating to the extent to which twins resembled one another physically, MZ twins were consistently viewed by their parents as more alike. The extent to which such external confusions became reflected in confusions about the twins' feelings about themselves, at least as far as these maternal reports are concerned, was only at the level of a trend ($p < .08$). The strength of these findings might be interpreted as supportive of the validity of the zygosity as designated by these mothers. They are consistent and quite strong. Further, mothers were not equally enthusiastic in rating each of the questions in a particular direction, which would suggest that mothers were not trying to create an impression of similarity for their identical twins.

Examples of affirmative answers to the question of whether the twins ever get confused as to whom they are included the following:

"Around twenty-four months both called each other [name of twin A] and wanted others to call them [name of twin A]."

"When asked who she was, one of my twins told the nursery lady, 'I don't know, I can't tell me apart.' They were two then, now four, they have no trouble."

"Ask, 'where is [twin A (or B)]?' They always point to themself. Looking in the mirror they always call the other's name."

Among the affirmative answers to the question, Do you or your husband ever mix them up? were the following:

"I put the wrong baby in the wrong bed and couldn't understand why they wouldn't go to sleep until my husband found the mistake.

He put them in the correct bed, and both immediately laid down and went to sleep."

"Once, when we were at the health clinic, I told the nurse that she had [twin B]. After putting all the information (weight, etc.) about the baby in [twin B's] chart, I discovered she had [twin A]."

"We often call them by the wrong name, especially if I don't have my glasses on."

"My husband always [mixes them up]. He tries to help me in feeding them. He feeds one and puts her down, and then he doesn't know which one he has fed."

"One morning I responded to one baby's cries, brought her into bed and nursed her and played with her. Then I discovered she was not whom I thought [she was] . . . It was a very strange feeling."

"I nursed one twice. Both of us mix them up only momentarily now."

"Father occasionally confused them when they were small infants, but never with any consequence other than one child drinking two bottles."

The descriptions given for both questions are supportive of some of the developmental formulations presented in earlier chapters, especially chapter 3. The parents are describing the difficulties that twins have in feeling separate from one another as well as the difficulties which others in their environment have in responding to them individually. These descriptions were especially true for MZ twins.

One of the ways in which such different perceptions might get played out would be in the extent to which twinness was accentuated by dressing the twins alike. As shown in table 7, there were no major differences among the three twin groups on the extent to which they were dressed alike, although DZOS twins tended to be dressed alike less frequently.

Table 8 reflects a series of questions relating to the twin relationship and parental treatment of them. Among the affirmative answers to the question regarding dependency were the following:

"[Twin B] seems to depend on [twin A] more. If she gets sent to the corner, he goes along. If she heads out across the yard next door, he follows along. She, however, does not look after him, but does want him around."

Table 7. *How Alike the Twins Dress*

	MZ	DZSS	DZOS
Have you ever dressed your twins alike?	90%	86%	73%
How often?			
Never	9%	20%	27%
Sometimes	56%	40%	59%
Very often	35%	40%	13%
Why do you dress them alike? (N = Sometimes + Often)			
Special outings	16%	19%	44%
Twins' choice	32%	21%	8%
Strangers curious about twins?	79%	76%	58%

Table 8. *Parental Treatment and Twin Dependency*

	Total	MZ	DZSS	DZOS
Are the twins treated equally? (yes)	19%	21%	25%	8%
Do the twins depend on each other?				
One depends more on the other	20%	15%	12%	30%
Both depend on each other	18%	17%	10%	10%
What is the twins' reaction to being separated from each other?				
Enjoy the independence		5%	3%	6%
Neutral		23%	19%	29%
Behavioral (ask for each other)		18%	31%	18%
Affective (get fussy or upset)		21%	25%	18%

"[Twin B] lets [twin A] speak for both."

"[Twin A] is having trouble adjusting to a new town and new school and looks to [twin B] for comfort. On other occasions, [twin B] has sought comfort from [twin A]."

"[Twin B] depends more on [twin A]. [Twin B] wants [twin A] to help him dress, make decisions at times."

"They alternate a lot of times. [Twin B] will send [twin A] to get things for her, and other times [twin B] will baby [twin A] and take care of her. [Twin A] is usually the one to take care of things."

"[Twin A] depends on her sister, who has a stronger character."

"[Twin A] does try to mother [twin B] when they are someplace, just the two of them and neither parent is around."

"[Twin B] is very much the leader, almost to the point of being bossy!"

These examples lend some support to the view that the twinship may serve a transitional function for some twins. They also underscore that in some twinships dependency has an early origin. Further, in chapter 6 it was suggested that sometimes each twin has a different level of investment in the relationship. Again, the examples support the view that such differential investment has an early origin as well.

Mothers were also asked the following question: What is the twins' reaction to being separated from each other?

Typical examples for mothers who said their twins did react to being separated from each other included the following:

"They haven't been separated much, but when they have, they walk around saying, 'Where [twin A] go?' They prefer being together to being separate."

"They are getting better. Separating them used to be like taking away a security blanket."

"Seem to rejoice when reunited after any period of about an hour or more apart."

"When one twin attends 'Mother's day out' without the other, they don't play as well and ask about the other's whereabouts frequently."

"Not much separation at this point. But they do prefer to sleep in one crib. I always place them in separate cribs, but they always get in the other's crib by the time I check them."

"Even at one year of age, when one is napping and the other isn't, the one who is awake goes around the house as if she were lost. She comes back to life when her sister awakes."

"When [twin B] was hospitalized earlier this year, both boys really missed each other . . . when they were reunited after ten days, they ran to each other and hugged forever! . . . during their separation [twin A] constantly called [twin B] on an imaginary phone and talked with him; [twin B] didn't mention [twin A]."

Table 9. Similarities and Differences

	Total	MZ	DZSS	DZOS
How do you see the twin relationship in the future?				
Close, loving	80%	78%	79%	85%
Competitive	2%	3%	2%	0
Protective	2%	3%	0	4%
Like siblings	34%	33%	40%	23%
How much rivalry exists between the twins? (average)				
(1 = never, 5 = always)		2.6	2.9	2.8
In terms of personality, how are the twins similar?				
Aggression		19%	6%	8%
Fussy		47%	50%	33%
Independent		25%	23%	8%
Social		40%	39%	58%
Activity level		13%	6%	0
Frequency of similarities cited (mean)		1.4	1.0	1.0
In terms of personality, how are the twins different?				
Aggression		46%	29%	42%
Fussy		46%	62%	58%
Independent		43%	43%	35%
Social		31%	43%	42%
Activity level		11%	17%	35%
Frequency of differences cited (mean)		1.7	1.8	2.1

Finally, mothers were asked, How do you see the twin relationship in the future? In terms of personality, how are the twins similar and how are they different? Table 9 provides a summary of their responses. One-way ANOVA's revealed no significant differences between MZ and DZ twins in terms of the reported frequency of similarities or differences.

The questions regarding similarities and differences are closely related to the genetic literature on personality since many of the same variables are under consideration. A quick glance would suggest that few of these characteristics seem to have a significant heritable component, since MZ and DZSS differences are modest at best. However, considerable caution is in order here. Most important, unlike the usual genetically oriented study, these questions were not objective; rather they were open-ended and self-reported. Few, if any, mothers actually mentioned every category noted under the similarity and difference questions. Thus these responses are not really comparable to those found in the literature more generally, even though they appear to refer to traits frequently noted in that literature. It is noteworthy that in the context of open-ended questions the adjectives that mothers spontaneously used to describe their twins were so similar to the traits habitually studied. This would suggest that there is some validity to the variables most frequently investigated.

Another major reservation requires consideration when interpreting these results. As Loehlin and Nichols (1976) point out, to assess adequately the heritable component in a given trait or behavior, a large sample is indispensable. The present sample is clearly not large enough to flesh out such differences. (It should be kept in mind that this survey was not designed to test for the extent of genetic contribution.) Nevertheless, it is interesting to note that if we simply take the raw number of similarities cited by mothers for each of the three twinship groups, the trend is in the direction that would be predicted by the genetic hypothesis (more similarities cited for MZ twins than for either DZSS or DZOS twins).

The survey results provide a picture of a number of variables which can be considered important in twin development. Probably the most important results are those relating to the early twin situation and the difficulties that twins frequently encounter during their first year. These include a high incidence of birth complications, prematurity and low birth weight, extended neonatal hospitalizations, and major illnesses during infancy. Prematurity has been linked to potential difficulties in infant-mother attachment, hence to potential difficulties in socioemotional development. Reports of frequency of twins seeking psychological help do not support the view that twins suffer more psychopathology (e.g., Joseph, 1961; Paluszny & Abelson, 1975) since they are not disproportionately represented in patient populations. Nevertheless, it is possible that nonspecific consequences of such developmental circumstances persist for some of those twins who fall in these at-risk categories (prematurity, low birth weight, major illness during first year of life). This is the position taken by Koch (1966). No doubt there must be wide variations here, depending on constitutional differences between twins, the sensitivity of doctors and hospital staff as well as the impact of these circumstances on parents' feelings about their twins.

The sheer extent to which these factors are at play in twinship raises major questions about twin-singleton comparisons in research or about the generalizability of studies involving twins to the population at large, since these results suggest major differences between twin and nontwin developmental environments during the first year of life. Such differences are rarely discussed by twin researchers who assume that, except for being twins, twin-singleton developmental contexts are comparable. Gottesman (1963), in his discussion of the limitations of the Twin Method, notes that the assumption that within-pair environmental variance is the same for MZ and DZSS twins may be questionable because some researchers (e.g., Price, 1950) have found differences between these two groups for such variables as fetal crowding and unequal distribution of fetal blood supply. Gottesman also notes, as is being suggested here, that twin researchers often overlook important postnatal differences between the two groups of twins (for example, the higher infant mortality rate for MZ twins would suggest other important physiological differences between MZ and DZ twins). Cohen, Dibble, Girawe, & Pollin (1975) have described these conditions as potentially detrimental to socioemotional development.

Perhaps more important is that for many of these variables (e.g., extra time in the hospital neonatally, length of that additional stay, major illness in infancy) there were important within-air differences *across* the three twinship groups. Further, though MZ twins were less different in terms of birth weight, there were noticeable differences in weight even with MZ twins. Numerous researchers have noted the tendency for parents of twins to focus on small differences in their twins and inflate these as a way of distinguishing them. To the extent that such differential perceptions, regardless of their lack of objectivity, affect parental treatment and attitudes toward each of their twins, the conditions are set for differences in the intrapair environments across twinship groups. However, most genetic researchers make the assumption that members of a twin pair share an equal environment—a questionable assumption. The results of this survey raise major questions about the validity of the equal-environments hypothesis in twin research.

8

Summary and Conclusions

Although twins have been the subject of considerable research, we know relatively little about the psychological characteristics of twins or the effects of the twin situation on their development. As Farber (1981) has noted, we lack an adequate conceptualization of twin development. This book provides such a conceptualization by drawing from existent developmental frameworks and evidence regarding the early experience of twins. The data presented here have provided a means through which specific issues in twinship can be viewed in relief. The twins' descriptions of their experience, in particular, permit a clear and vivid image of what being a twin is really like and of the feelings, thoughts, and concerns that twins have about themselves and each other.

The present work emphasizes the extent to which twinship constitutes a specific developmental context which alters the usual circumstances governing development. Both the twin interviews and the mothers-of-twins data support this conclusion. It has been shown, for example, that the first year of life is often stressful and difficult for twins. Almost half of the mothers surveyed reported their twins to be less than five and a half pounds at birth, for example, a circumstance frequently associated with a variety of medical difficulties and some psychological difficulties as well. Further, a large proportion of these twins required hospitalization postnatally for at least several weeks, and many had major medical problems during their first year of life. A high proportion of the mothers reported pregnancy complications while carrying their twins as well. Together, these circumstances form a clear picture: twinship must be considered an at-risk developmental situation. This is especially true when one considers the added difficulties of parenting two infants at the same time. The reports from the mothers of twins were consistent in their descriptions of how taxing and difficult it was for them to manage twin infants, especially during their first year. The mothers experienced constant exhaustion because the twins' incessant demands did not allow them to get much sleep. In this context, it is understandable that the mother of twins may have little or no energy available to help her twins overcome their own stresses.

Although not all twins encounter the neonatal or postnatal problems just described, and not all mothers of twins feel as overwhelmed by the needs of two infants, the data presented in chapter 7 in particular illustrate how prevalent these stresses are. The intent here is not to paint a bleak picture of the twin situation, but to underscore that, even in the best of circumstances, it can be a difficult task to tend to the needs of two infants at once and that these difficulties give the developmental context of twinship a particular character.

From a developmental perspective, these circumstances must be looked at carefully in terms of their potential effects on twin children. We have theoretical reasons to believe that the twin situation may affect socioemotional development in a variety of ways. For instance, numerous theorists (e.g., Ainsworth, 1964, 1967, 1969; Mahler, 1963, 1968; Mahler et al., 1975; Brazelton et al., 1975) have discussed the importance of the quality of parent-infant interaction during the first year of life for establishing a secure base for subsequent socioemotional development. From a very early age infants are capable of entering into rather complex interactive patterns with others in their environment. The quality of such interactions has been related experimentally to subsequent psychological development. They have been linked, for example, to a longer attention span in infants (Brody, 1956) and to the quality of a child's attachment to the mother during the first year (e.g., Ainsworth, 1969). Quality of attachment has also been related to variations in later development (e.g., Matas et al. 1978; Arend et al., 1979). Thus, the nature of parent-child interactions is of considerable importance.

Good quality interactions are those in which the parent is able to respond adequately to an infant's need states. During a relatively short span of time, an infant may traverse several such need states—hunger, sleepiness, being in need of changing, alertness and in need of stimulation, or fatigue and in need of a reduction in the amount of stimulation. A parent must be capable of adequately sensing the infant's different states to be able to appropriately engage the infant. The capacity of a parent to respond effectively to variations in an infant's need states can be interfered with in a number of ways. Some parents are not able to respond to their infant adequately because their feelings simply get in the way. In other words, their own psychological organization precludes this. Other parents are capable of sensing and responding to their infant, but life events interfere. For example, if a mother has suffered a loss around the time of the birth of her child, her depression may make it difficult for her to be responsive to her infant in the same way that she would otherwise have been. Similarly, the parent who is chronically tired and feels drained by the incessant demands of two infants might well find it more difficult to maintain an optimal level of responsivity. Research has shown that parents of twins tend to interact less with their twin children than do parents of single children (e.g., Gosher-Gottstein, 1979; Lytton, 1980). In considering these twin-singleton comparisons, Lytton concluded that twinship constitutes an enduring ecological factor that has considerable impact on twin development.

It is important to recognize that considerable variation is to be expected regarding any particular twin situation. Such issues as whether either of the twins required postnatal hospitalization or whether there were major medical problems are important. The innate constitution of the twins is also important, as are the number and ages of other children already in the household and especially the amount of support available to the parents of twins. All of these variables help to determine what the particular reality of the twin situation is like. These variables also have a direct effect on the degree of stress or the amount of frustration which twins experience and, in turn, on the extent to which twin socioemotional development is affected by them.

What has been described in this book is a developmental context to which twins must adapt, a context that is defined by the particulars of the twin situation. Every family represents a unique and specific setting that is structured by its members and the circumstances in which they live. These factors affect the development of the child, giving a particular cast to that child's psychology. In this sense twinship constitutes an important part of a twin's adaptational context. Twinship is part of the psychological reality governing the twin's life, and thus, over time, it becomes part of a twin's internalized reality, part of the twin's personality organization. That it is possible to detect certain issues which characterize twin psychology does not speak to the extent to which a twin's development has or has not been compromised. Although the psychological risks inherent in twinship have been emphasized in this book, it is not the intention here to depict twins in psychopathological terms. However, it does a disservice to twins and to their parents to minimize the real challenges created by the circumstance of twinship. A realistic perception of these difficulties, as well as a realistic view of what is at stake in how these difficulties are handled, actually facilitates the efforts of those interested in optimizing twin development.

Three potential stress points in twin development have been suggested here. The first, implicit in the preceding discussion, occurs during the first six months of life in what Mahler (1968) terms the normal symbiotic phase. An adequate affective coupling between parent and infant is all-important. As noted, the danger is that a parent of twins may feel too depleted to respond adequately to each twin infant.

The second stress point occurs during what Mahler et al. (1975) term the rapprochement subphase of separation-individuation, when the twin infant is roughly between eighteen months and twenty-four months. The process of developing a sense of oneself as a separate, autonomous individual is at times stressful for all children, since it implies the loss of the nurturant and comforting experiences characteristic of infancy. For this reason, rapprochement constitutes a crisis of sorts for every child, as the child struggles with countervailing and simultaneous wishes to be independent *and* to remain dependent.

The process of differentiation in twins is complicated for two reasons. First, if the normal symbiotic phase was characterized by excessive frustration, the psychological resources that are required for separation-individuation may not be fully available. Second, there may be an excessive degree of intertwin identification. One source of this interidentification may be fostered unwittingly by parents who, after a period of considerable demands and sleepless nights, find it a welcome relief for the twins to begin entertaining and comforting each other. The natural tendency for children of this age to turn to transitional objects to dilute the stresses of separation-individuation also plays an important role. Other persons contribute to this process as well, through their natural and spontaneous reactions to twins. Such circumstances serve to cement the twin relationship as a psychologically vital tie that is more intense than the usual sibling relationship. (As evidenced by the differences in the frequency with which others became confused about the twins' identity, described in chapter 7, this is one arena in which the experience of identical twins may be somewhat more complicated than that of fraternal twins.) However, excessive intertwin identification can interfere with the process of separation-individuation which culminates with the rapprochement crisis. Unlike the singleton, twins are faced with a dual task in separation-individuation: they must attain a degree of differentiation from both *mother* and *twin*. Both tasks are difficult to attain, and intertwin identification and social expectations regarding the closeness of twins serve to reinforce the twin relationship.

These circumstances lead directly to the third difficult developmental juncture for many twins: adolescence. As Blos (1967) has noted, in many respects adolescence is best thought of as a second separation-individuation. Many of the same psychological issues that characterize separation-individuation are reworked during adolescence, with separation from the family as the crucial developmental task. To the extent that a cohesive sense of identity is only tenuously established, adolescence can be a period of unusual stress. Often, the struggle to differentiate from one's twin, which may have been in a state of moratorium from the first separation-individuation, surfaces directly as a developmental challenge. Thus, as was true during the first separation-individuation, twins are again faced with a double task in adolescence; they must individuate from the family as well as from the twin relationship. However, during adolescence it is considerably more difficult to use the twin relationship transitionally—that is, as a way of diluting the impact of the developmental tasks at hand.

Prototypical adolescent activities, such as developing best friends with whom one shares intimate secrets, closely parallel the twin relationship itself. This similarity can create major tensions, as twins attempt to redefine the nature of their relationship. At the same time, the peer group in adolescence may place more expectations on twins to function independently than is true within the twins' family. Within the family, twinship is a fact of life and accommodations are made to it. Such accommodations may be harder to come by in the peer group where modes of relating that are not defined by family contexts are the norm. The expectation that one should function independently places an added stress on the twin relationship. As we have seen in earlier chapters, twins often feel ambivalent about this process: they *wish* to individuate (and may feel guilty for these feelings) but also feel vulnerable to the experience of losing someone who means a great deal to them.

In adulthood one sees a broad range of relationships between twins. Some twins in this project appeared to be actively involved in resolving the issues associated with the twin relationship. This fact alone is a testament to the power of the twin relationship. In other twinships, there was no longer an active struggle to sort out these issues. The relationship that twins develop with one another is clearly important. Leonard (1961) noted that from the age of about six months twins are aware of each other's presence and can have a soothing effect on one another. In the adult interviews that comprised this project, it was possible to see that these characteristics of the twin relationship extend well beyond infancy. Numerous twins described the soothing and comforting feelings associated with having one's twin present during difficult periods. These observations seemed somewhat independent of the extent to which twins were manifestly involved in one another's lives. Across twinships one could readily see the enduring importance of that relationship in their lives.

What are the characteristic twin issues that have been identified in this work? The material presented supports the commonly held view that twins frequently encounter difficulties in identity consolidation. There were various ways in which such difficulties were evident. The clearest, however, were those statements by twins themselves in which they described transient feelings that *who* they were was in jeopardy. Statements indicating that too much time spent with one's twin resulted in the feeling that one's sense of self was threatened with dissolution would be one such example. On the other hand, numerous twins described the sense that without their co-twin they felt themselves to be *incomplete* as persons. Sometimes both of these sentiments were voiced by the same twin, reflecting the complexity of the issues involved.

Concerns regarding identity formation presented themselves in a variety of other ways as well. One illustration of this phenomenon is the rigid role complementarity which was found in many twinships. Here, aspects of identity appeared to be carved out such that each twin had a clearly defined area of talent, activity, or interest. The rigidity of such areas of differentiation is what renders them suspect. In some instances, one of the twins later refused to remain restricted to the previously agreed on lines of demarcation, but such decisions were only made with a great deal of difficulty.

There is considerable evidence, both experimental and clinical, that many twins develop differential relationships with their parents. In this sample of twins, the reasons for such differential relationships were varied. At times these seemed to be related to real, observable characteristics of the twins themselves. For example, one twin might be more robust than another, a factor influencing subsequent alignment with one parent or the other. In other circumstances, however, the real characteristics of the twins appeared to play a relatively minor role. This appeared to be the case in twinships in which the names chosen for each twin prenatally were clearly important to the parents in ways that seemed to play a part in differential parent-twin relationships postnatally.

Some of the difficulties related to identity consolidation in twinship must be inferred. For example, the data from the twin interviews illustrates aspects of the twin relationship, such as dependency and separation anxiety, which can be readily understood in terms of the cohesiveness of the self. To the extent that the integration of various dimensions of a twin's personality is incomplete, a wide range of activities that fall under the general rubric of autonomous functioning can be affected. One could observe in a number of the twins who participated in this project a marked reliance on the twinship. In this context, threats to the intertwin relationship were experienced as direct threats to the cohesion of the self.

Perhaps one of the most poignant dimensions of the twin relationship is the discrepancy between twins' sense of what twin relationships are supposed to be like, as contrasted with the reality of their own relationships. Throughout history, and in contemporary culture as well, people have had strong reactions to twinship. The twin relationship has been the source of considerable fantasy, as others have sought to find in it idealized qualities missing in their own lives and relationships. It is true that the twin relationship is, generally speaking, somewhat more intense than that ordinarily found between siblings. Yet, it is also true that the twin relationship does not conform to the expectations that are often placed at its doorstep.

Virtually all of the subjects interviewed were acutely aware of what "real twins" were supposed to be like—uniquely close, especially communicative, and attuned to each other's feelings and needs. However, in every instance their own relationship fell short of such high expectations. The number of subjects who voiced disappointment at the level of closeness in their twin relationship was in marked contrast to others' expectations of the twin relationship. Twins appear to encounter the same difficulties as nontwins do in relationships that have important emotional value. However, such a real-world quality has different implications in the context of the twin relationship, since twins *believe* that their relationship should be uniquely close. As seen in chapter 6, most twins concluded that their own twin relationship was more like ordinary siblings than a twin relationship, since it was missing that special, idealized closeness. Such discrepancies between expectation and reality result in disappointment.

Finally, the present study raised a number of questions regarding the basic assumptions underlying the Twin Method. First, the prevalence of neonatal and postnatal difficulties for twin infants, including those associated with the low birth weight, pose problems for twin-singleton comparisons and for the generalization of findings from twin data to nontwin populations. In addition, findings regarding differences in parent-infant interaction for twins versus singletons suggest that the environments are not generally comparable. The assumption that the presence of two infants has only negligible effects on development is questionable.

In genetic research, twin-twin comparisons are the most common, since MZ and DZSS twins are usually compared. The assumption is that members of a twin pair share an environment which is, for all intents and purposes, the same. But is this really the case? The detailed exploration of the lives of these subjects raises questions regarding this assumption as well. Many aspects of the environment for a pair of twins are often the same: They are raised in the same household, which means that they share the same socioeconomic status. They have the same parents and the same number of siblings. The twins are of the same age, which means that they move through developmental steps roughly at the same time, and so forth. Without question, the twin situation offers more control over extraneous variables than would be true for other sibling comparisons.

The differences here, however, are especially important. For example, the data on rigid role complementarity suggest that the twin situation may artificially accentuate psychological processes which are at play within the family. Further, the interview data convincingly show that the twins' relationships with important people in their environment can be quite different. As has been noted, twins often have different relationships with each parent and sometimes different relationships with the mother in particular. More controlled observations have led to similar conclusions. For example, Lytton (1980) found that a significant subset of his sample had differential attachments to each of the parents. The findings of Plomin and Rowe (1979), in which MZ twins differed considerably in the quality of attachment to their mothers, also support the conclusion that each member of the twin pair can evolve a different relationship with the mother. Thus, there is good evidence, both interview-derived and experimental, in support of the notion that twins do not share the same quality of relationship with important people in their environment. The interviews show that these become translated into important differences between twins which are sustained into adulthood. The assumptions of the Twin Method require that we view these differences as minimal. However, these differences contribute in substantive ways to the personality organization of twins and therefore must be appreciated.

The data that comprise this project pose a more extreme question to genetic researchers. Historically, twin researchers set out to understand their subject in a more comprehensive manner. The classic work of Newman and colleagues (1937) is an excellent illustration. These researchers approached their subject matter with a multitude of measures but *also* with a multitude of methods! They were equally comfortable administering a set of scales as they were interviewing their subjects about a variety of life experiences. Newman et al. did not shy away from sharing personal impressions hand in hand with descriptions of statistical procedures. Their work is impressive in part because one can see the researchers grappling with the complexities of the questions before them in a three-dimensional manner.

Much contemporary psychological research, twin or otherwise, has lost this vision. Yet, in the present context one can readily see what is lost. Present-day genetic researchers often approach the twin subject with the sterility of the surgeon. Instruments are administered whose connection to real-life psychological processes, experiences, or perceptions is often not really understood. Correlations are presented with authority, while the content to which they refer remains elusive. There is no doubt in my mind that genetic factors play a part in human development; however, to be of value, genetic research must do more than present significant correlations. The factors that these researchers investigate, regardless of how often the results are replicated, must ultimately be related to real-life events and experiences. As one reads the material from the subjects' interviews, one is struck by the differences in twins' lives. Further, these differences are in important and substantive areas. Assessments of the genetic inheritability of psychological traits must be integrated with the differences that one finds on closer inspection of twins' lives. Although some might dismiss such approaches as impressionistic and anecdotal, day-to-day life must be the ultimate testing ground for theoretical constructs.

Selected Bibliography

Ackerman, P. H. (1975). Narcissistic personality disorder in an identical twin. *International Journal of Psychoanalytic Psychotherapy*, 4, 389–409.

Ainslie, R. C. (1979). Separation-individuation and the psychology of twinship (Doctoral Dissertation, University of Michigan, 1979). *Dissertation Abstracts International*, 40(5).

Ainslie, R. C., & Nagera, H. (1980). *How children enter treatment.* Unpublished manuscript.

Ainsworth, M. D. S. (1964). Patterns of attachment behavior shown by the infant in interaction with his mother. *Merrill-Palmer Quarterly*, 10, 51–58.

Ainsworth, M. D. S. (1967). *Infancy in Uganda: Infant care and the growth of love.* Baltimore: Johns Hopkins University Press.

Ainsworth, M. D. S. (1969). Object relations, dependency, and attachment: A theoretical review of the infant-mother relationship. *Child Development*, 40, 969–1025.

Ainsworth, M. D. S. (1972). Attachment and dependency: A comparison. In S. L. Gewirtz (Ed.), *Attachment and dependency*. New York: Wiley.

Ainsworth, M. D. S., & Bell, S. M. (1974). Mother-infant interaction and the development of competence. In K. J. Connolly & J. Bruner (Eds.), *The growth of competence*. New York: Academic Press.

Ainsworth, M. D. S., Blehar, M. C., Waters, E., & Wall, S. (1978). *Patterns of attachment: A psychological study of the strange situation.* Hillsdale, NJ: Lawrence Erlbaum.

Allen, M. G., Greenspan, S. I, & Pollin, W. (1976). The effect of parental perceptions on early development in twins. *Psychiatry*, *39*, 65–71.

Allen, M. G., Pollin, W., & Hoffer, A. (1971). Parental, birth, and infancy factors in twin development. *American Journal of Psychiatry*, *127*, 1597–1604.

Amsterdam, D. (1972). Mirror self-image reactions before age two. *Developmental Psychology*, *5*, 297–305.

Arend, R., Gove, F. L., & Sroufe, L. A. (1979). Infancy to kindergarten: A predictive study of ego-resiliency and curiosity in preschoolers. *Child Development*, *50*, 950–959.

Arlow, J. (1960). Fantasy systems in twins. *Psychoanalytic Quarterly*, *29*, 175–199.

Askevoid, F., & Heiberg, A. (1979). Anorexia nervosa: Two cases in discordant MZ twins. *Psychotherapy and Psychosomatics*, *32*, 223–228.

Babson, S. G. & Phillips, D. S. (1973). Growth and development of twins dissimilar in size at birth. *New England Journal of Medicine*, *289*, 937–940.

Barden, T. P. (1983). Premature labor. In A. A. Fanaroff & R. J. Martin (Eds.), *Behman's neonatal-perinatal medicine: Diseases of the fetus and infant* (3rd ed.). St. Louis: C. V. Mosby.

Barr, A., & Stevenson, A. C. (1961). Stillbirths and infant mortality in twins. *Annual of Human Genetics*, *25*, 131–140.

Basit, A. (1972). A Rorschach study of personality development in identical and fraternal twins. *Journal of Personality Assessment*, *36*, 23–27.

Benirschke, K. (1983). Placental pathology. In A. A. Fanaroff & R. J. Martin (Eds.), *Behman's neonatal-perinatal medicine: Diseases of the fetus and infant* (3rd ed.). St. Louis: C. V. Mosby.

Berlyne, D. E. (1960). *Conflict, arousal, and curiosity*. New York: McGraw-Hill.

Bernstein, B. A. (1980). Siblings of twins. *Psychoanalytic Study of the Child*, *35*, 135–154.

Bibring, G. (1959). Some considerations of the psychological processes of pregnancy. *Psychoanalytic Study of the Child*, *14*, 113–121.

Bibring, G., Dwyer, T., Huntington, D., & Valenstein, S. (1961). A study of the psychological process in pregnancy and of the earliest mother-child relationship. *Psychoanalytic Study of the Child*, 20, 9–72.

Blewett, D. B. (1954). An experimental study of the inheritance of intelligence. *Journal of Mental Science*, 100, 922–933.

Blos, P. (1967). The second individuation process in adolescence. *Psychoanalytic Study of the Child*, 22, 162–186.

Blos, P. (1970). *The young adolescent: Clinical studies*. New York: The Free Press.

Bowlby, J. (1969). *Attachment*. New York: Basic Books.

Brazelton, T. B., Koslowski, B., & Main, M. (1974). The origins of reciprocity: The early mother-infant interaction. In M. Lewis & L. A. Rosenblum (Eds.), *The effect of the infant on its caregiver*. New York: Wiley-Interscience.

Brazelton, T. B., Tronick, E., Adamson, L., Als, H., & Wise, S. (1975). Early mother-infant reciprocity. In Ciba Foundation Symposium 33, *Parent-infant interaction*. New York: Elsevier North-Holland, 137–154.

Breland, H. M. (1973). Birthorder effects: A reply to Schooler. *Psychological Bulletin*, 80, 210–212.

Brody, D. (1937). Twin resemblances in mechanical ability, with reference to the effects of practice on performance. *Child Development*, 8, 207–216.

Brody, S. (1956). *Patterns of mothering: Maternal influence during infancy*. New York: International Universities Press.

Brown, A. M., Stafford, R. E., & Vandenberg, G. (1967). Twins: behavioral differences. *Child Development*, 38, 1055–1064.

Burlingham, D. (1945). The fantasy of having a twin. *Psychoanalytic Study of the Child*, 1, 205–210.

Burlingham, D. (1946). Twins: observations of environmental influences on their development. *Psychoanalytic Study of the Child*, 2, 61–73.

Burlingham, D. (1949). The relationship of twins to each other. *Psychoanalytic Study of the Child*, 3 & 4, 57–72.

Burlingham, D. (1952). *Twins, a study of three pairs of identical twins*. London: Imago.

Burt, C. (1966). The genetic determination of differences in intelligence: A study of monozygotic twins reared together and apart. *British Journal of Psychology*, 57, 137–153.

Buss, A. H., & Plomin, R. A. (1975). *Temperament theory of personality development.* New York: Wiley.

Buss, A. H., Plomin, R., & Willerman, L. (1973). The inheritance of temperaments. *Journal of Personality, 41,* 513–524.

Canter, S. (1973). Personality traits in twins. In G. E. Claridge, S. Canter, & W. I. Hume (Eds.). *Personality differences and biological variations: A study of twins.* Oxford, NY: Pergamon Press.

Carter, H. D. (1935). Twin similarities in emotional traits. *Character and Personality, 4,* 61–78.

Carter-Saltzman, L., Scarr-Salapatek, S. (1975). Blood group, behavioral, and morphological differences among dizygotic twins. *Social Biology, 22,* 372–374.

Cattell, R. B., Blewett, D. B., & Beleff, J. R. (1955). The inheritance of personality. A multiple variance analysis determination of approximate nature-nurture ratios for primary personality factors in Q-data. *American Journal of Human Genetics, 7,* 122–146.

Cederloff, R., Frieberg, L., Jonson, E., & Kaij, L. (1961). Studies of similarity diagnosis in twins with the aid of mailed questionnaires. *Acta Genetica, 11,* 338–362.

Claridge, G. E., Canter, S., & Hume, W. I. (1973). *Personality differences and biological variations: A study of twins.* Oxford, NY: Pergamon Press.

Cohen, D. J., Allen, M. G., Pollin, M. D., Inoff, G., Werner, A., & Dibble, E. (1972). Personality development in twins: Competence in the newborn and preschool periods. *Journal of the American Academy of Child Psychiatry, 11,* 625–644.

Cohen, D. J., Dibble, E., & Grawe, J. M. (1977). Father's and mother's perceptions of children's personality. *Archives of General Psychiatry, 34,* 480–487.

Cohen, D. J., Dibble, E., Grawe, J. M., & Pollin, W. (1975). Reliably separating identical from fraternal twins. *Archives of General Psychiatry, 32,* 1371–1375.

Cohen, S. E., & Beckwith, L. (1979). Preterm-infant interactions with caregivers in the first year of life and competence at age two. *Child Development, 50,* 767–776.

Condon, W. & Sander, L. (1974). Synchrony demonstrated between movements of the neonate and adult speech. *Child Development, 45,* 456–462.

Conway, D., Lytton, H., & Pysh, F. (1980). Twin-singleton language differences. *Canadian Journal of Behavioral Science, 12,* 264–271.

Coombs, D. F. (1978). *The psychology of twins.* Unpublished manuscript.

Costello, A. (1975). Are mothers stimulating? In R. Lewin (Ed.). *Child Alive.* London: Temple Smith.

Cronin, H. (1933). An analysis of the neuroses of identical twins. *Psychoanalytic Review, 20,* 375–387.

Day, E. (1932) The development of language in twins: Comparison of twins and single children. *Child Development, 3,* 179–199.

Demarest, E., & Winestine, M. (1955). The initial phase of concomitant treatment of twins. *Psychoanalytic Study of the Child, 10,* 336–352.

Deutsch, H. (1938). Folie à deux. *Psychoanalytic Quarterly, 7,* 307–318.

Dustman, R. E., & Beck, E. C. (1965). The visual evoked response in twins: Electro-encephalogram. *Clinical Neurophysiology, 19,* 570–575.

Dworkin, R. H. (1979). Genetic and environmental influences on person-situation interactions. *Journal of Research in Personality, 13,* 279–293.

Dworkin, R. H., Burke, B. W., Maher, B. A., & Gottesman, I. I. (1977). Genetic influences on the organization and development of personality. *Developmental Psychology, 13,* 164–165.

Engel, G. L. (1975). The death of a twin: Mourning and anniversary reactions. Fragments of ten years of self-analysis. *International Journal of Psycho-Analysis, 56,* 23–40.

Erikson, E. H. (1950). *Childhood and society.* New York: W. W. Norton.

Erikson, E. H. (1968). *Identity youth and crisis.* New York: W. W. Norton.

Erlenmeyer-Kimling, L., & Jarvik, L. F. 1963. Genetics and intelligence. *Science, 142,* 1477–1479.

Escalona, S. (1963). Patterns of experience and the developmental process. *Psychoanalytic Study of the Child, 8,* 197–244.

Escalona, S. (1968). *The roots of individuality: Normal patterns of development in infancy.* Chicago: Adeline.

178

Eysenck, H. J. (1951). Neuroticism in twins. *Eugenics Review*, 43, 79–82.

Eysenck, H. J. (1956). The inheritance and nature of extraversion. *Eugenics Review*, 48, 23–30.

Eysenck, H. J., & Prell, D. B. (1951). The inheritance of neuroticism: An experimental study. *Journal of Mental Science*, 97, 441–465.

Falbo, T. (1982). Only children in America. In M. Lamb & B. Sutton-Smith (Eds.), *Sibling relationships*. Hillsdale, NJ: Erlbaum.

Fanaroff, A. A., & Martin, R. J. (Eds.). (1983). *Behman's neonatal-perinatal medicine: Diseases of the fetus and infant* (3rd ed.). St. Louis: C. V. Mosby.

Farber, S. L. (1981). *Identical twins reared apart: A reanalysis*. New York: Basic Books.

Field, T. M., Walden, T., Widmayer, S., & Breenbery, R. (1975). The early development of preterm, discordant twin pairs: Bigger is not always better. In L. P. Lipsitt & T. M. Field (Eds.), *Infant behavior and development: Perinatal risk and newborn behavior*. Norwood, NJ: Ablex.

Fraiberg, S. (1959). *The magic years*. New York: Scribners.

Fraiberg, S. (1969). Libidinal object constancy and mental representation. *Psychoanalytic Study of the Child*, 14, 9–47.

Fraiberg, S. (Ed.). (1980). *Clinical studies in infant mental health: The first year of life*. New York: Basic Books.

Freedman, D. (1965). An ethological approach to the genetical study of human behavior. In S. Vandenberg (Ed.), *Methods and goals in human behavior genetics*. New York: Academic Press.

Freedman, D. G., & Keller, B. (1963). Inheritance of behavior in infants. *Science*, 140, 196–198.

Freud, A. (1936). *The ego and the mechanisms of defense*. London: Hogarth Press.

Freud, A. (1965). *Normality and pathology of development in childhood: Assessments of development*. New York: International Universities Press.

Freud, A. (1981). *Psychoanalytic psychology of normal development*. New York: International Universities Press.

Freud, S. (1916). Introductory lectures on psychoanalysis. In *Stan-*

dard Edition, Vols. 15–16, edited by J. Strachey. London: Hogarth Press, 1963.

Freud, S. (1915). Mourning and melancholia. In *Standard Edition*, Vol. 14, edited by J. Strachey. London: Hogarth Press, 1957, 237–260.

Freud, S. (1900). *Interpretation of dreams*. In *Standard Edition*, Vols. 4–5, edited by J. Strachey. London: Hogarth Press, 1953.

Fuller, J. L., & Thompson, W. R. (1978). *Foundations of behavior genetics*. St. Louis: C. V. Mosby.

Gesell, A. (1931). The developmental psychology of twins. In C. Murchison (Ed.), *A handbook of child psychology*. Worcester, MA: Clark University Press.

Gesell, A. L., & Thompson, H. (1941). Twins T. and C. from infancy to adolescence: A biogenetic study of individual differences by the method of co-twin control. In C. Murchison (Ed.), *Genetic psychology monographs*. Provincetown, MA: Journal Press.

Gifford, S. B., Muraski, T., Brazelton, T. B., & Young, G. (1966). Differences in individual development within a pair of identical twins. *International Journal of Psychoanalysis*, 47, 261–268.

Glenn, J. (1966). Opposite sex twins. *Psychoanalytic Quarterly*, 34, 636–638.

Glenn, J. (1974a). Anthony and Peter Shaffer's plays: The influence of twinship on creativity. *American Imago*, 31, 270–292.

Glenn, J. (1974b). Twins in disguise: A psychoanalytic essay on "Sleuth and the Royal Hunt of the Sun." *Psychoanalytic Quarterly*, 43, 288–302.

Gosher-Gottstein, E. R. (1979). Families of twins: A longitudinal study of coping. *Twins: Newsletter of the International Society for Twin Studies*, 4–5, 2.

Gottesman, I. I. (1963). Heritability of personality: A demonstration. *Psychological Monographs*, 77 (Serial No. 572).

Gottesman, I. I. (1966). Genetic variance in an adaptive personality trait. *Journal of Child Psychology and Psychiatry*, 7, 199–208.

Gottesman, I. I., & Shields, J. (1972). *Schizophrenia and genetics: A twin study vantagepoint*. New York: Academic Press.

Gough, H. G. (1960). The adjective check list as a personality assessment research technique. *Psychological Reports*, 6, 107–122.

Graham, P., Rutter, M., & George, S. (1973). Temperamental characteristics as predictors of behavior disorders in children. *American Journal of Orthopsychiatry*, *43*, 328–339.

Greulich, W. W. (1934). Heredity in human twinning. *American Journal of Physical Anthropology*, *19*, 391–431.

Gross, S., Shurin, S., & Gordon, E. (1983). The blood and hematopoietic system. In A. A. Fanaroff & R. J. Martin (Eds.), *Behman's neonatal-perinatal medicine: Diseases of the fetus and infant* (3rd ed.). St. Louis: C. V. Mosby.

Hartmann, H. (1958). *Ego psychology and the problem of adaptation*. New York: International Universities Press.

Hartmann, H. (1964). *Essays on ego psychology*. New York: International Universities Press.

Hayes, R. F., & Bronzaft, A. L. (1979). Birth order and related variables in an academically elite sample. *Journal of Individual Psychology*, *35*, 214–234.

Hock, E., Coady, S., & Cordero, L. (1973, March). *Patterns of attachment to mother of one-year-old infants: A comparative study of full-term infants and prematurely born infants who were hospitalized throughout the neonatal period*. Paper presented at the meeting of the Society for Research in Child Development, Philadelphia.

Hoffman, J. A., & Teyber, E. D. (1979). Some relationships between sibling age, spacing and personality. *Merrill-Palmer Quarterly*, *25*, 77–80.

Horn, J. M., Plomin, R., & Rosenman, R. (1976). Heritability of personality traits in adult male twins. *Behavior Genetics*, *6*, 17–30.

Jacobson, E. (1954). The self and the object world. *Psychoanalytic Study of the Child*, *9*, 75–127.

Jinks, J. L., & Fulker, D. W. (1970). Comparisons of the biometrical genetical, MAVA, and classical approaches to the analysis of human behavior. *Psychological Bulletin*, *73*, 311–349.

Joseph, E. (1959). An unusual fantasy in a twin with an inquiry into the nature of fantasy. *Psychoanalytic Quarterly*, *28*, 189–206.

Joseph, E. (1961). The psychology of twins. *Journal of the American Psychoanalytic Association*, *9*, 158–166.

Joseph, E., & Tabor, J. (1961). The simultaneous analysis of a pair of identical twins and the twinning reaction. *Psychoanalytic Study of the Child*, *16*, 275–299.

Kagan, J., & Moss, H. (1962). *From birth to maturity*. New York: Wiley.

Kallmann, F. J. (1959). Psychogenetic studies of twins. In S. Koch (Ed.), *Psychology: A study of a science: Vol. 3. Formulations of the person and the social context*. New York: McGraw-Hill.

Kaplan, D., & Mason, E. (1960). Maternal reactions to premature birth viewed as an acute emotional disorder. *American Journal of Orthopsychiatry*, *30*, 539–549.

Kaplan, L. (1978). *Oneness and separateness: From infant to individual*. New York: Simon & Schuster.

Karn, M. N. (1953). Twin data: A further study of birth weight, gestation time, maternal age, order of birth, and survival. *Annual of Eugenics*, *17*, 233–248.

Karpman, B. (1953). Psychodynamics in a fraternal twinship relation. *Psychoanalytic Review*, *40*, 243–267.

Kernberg, O. (1966). Structural derivatives of object relations. *International Journal of Psycho-Analysis*, *47*, 236–253.

Kernberg, O. (1975). *Borderline conditions and pathological narcissism*. New York: Jason Aronson.

Kernberg, O. (1976). *Object-relations theory and clinical psychoanalysis*. New York: Jason Aronson.

Kim, L. L., Dales, R. J., Connor, R., Walters, J., & Witherspoon, R. (1969). Social interaction of like-sex twins and singletons in relation to intelligence, language, and physical development. *Journal of Genetic Psychology*, *114*, 203–214.

Klaus, M. H. & Fanaroff, A. A. (Eds.). (1973). *The care of the high-risk neonate*. Philadelphia: W. B. Saunders.

Klaus, M. H., & Kennel, J. (1973). Care of the mother. In Klaus, M. H. & Fanaroff, A. A. (Eds.), *The care of the high-risk neonate*. Philadelphia: W. B. Saunders.

Koch, H. L. (1964). A Study of twins born at different levels of maturity. *Child Development*, *35*, 1265–1282.

Koch, H. L. (1966). *Twins and twin relations*. Chicago: University of Chicago Press.

Kringlen, E. (1967). *Heredity and environment in the functional psychoses: An epidemiological-clinical study*. London: Heinemann Medical.

Lassers, E., & Nordan, R. (1978). Separation-individuation of an identical twin. *Adolescent Psychiatry*, *6*, 469–479.

Legg, C., Sherick, I., & Wadland, W. (1974). Reaction of preschool children to the birth of a sibling. *Child Psychiatry and Human Development*, 5, 3–39.

Leonard, M. (1961). Problems in identification and ego development in twins. *Psychoanalytic Study of the Child*, 16, 300–320.

Lichtenberg, J. (1975). The development of the sense of self. *Journal of the American Psychoanalytic Association*, 23, 453–484.

Lipsitt, L. P., & Field, T. M. (Eds.). (1969). *Infant behavior and development: Perinatal risk and newborn behavior*. Norwood, NJ: Ablex.

Loehlin, J. (1969). Psychological genetics. In R. Cattell (Ed.), *Handbook of modern personality theory*. New York: Adeline.

Loehlin, J. (1978). Are CPI scales differently heritable: How good is the evidence? *Behavior Genetics*, 8, 381–382.

Loehlin, J. G., & Nichols, R. C. (1976). *Heredity, environment, and personality: A study of 850 sets of twins*. Austin: University of Texas Press.

Luria, A. R., & Yudovitch, F. I. (1959). *Speech development of mental processes in the child*. London: Staple Press.

Lykken, D. T. (1978). The diagnosis of zygosity in twins. *Behavior Genetics*, 8, 437–473.

Lykken, D. T., Tellegen, A., & DeRubeis, R. (1978). Volunteer bias in twin research: The rule of two-thirds. *Social Biology*, 25, 1–9.

Lytton, H. (1977). Do parents create, or respond to, differences in twins? *Developmental Psychology*, 13, 456–459.

Lytton, H. (1980). *Parent-child interaction: The socialization process observed in twin and singleton families*. New York: Plenum.

Lytton, H., Conway, D., & Sauve, R. (1977). The impact of twinship on parent-child interaction. *Journal of Personality and Social Psychology*, 35, 97–107.

Lytton, H., Martin, N. B., & Eaves, L. (1977). Environmental and genetical causes of variation in ethological aspects of behavior in two-year-old boys. *Social Biology*, 24, 200–211.

Maechen, A. (1968). Object cathexis in a borderline twin. *Psychoanalytic Study of the Child*, 23, 438–456.

Mahler, M. (1958). On two crucial phases of integration of the source of identity: Separation-individuation and bisexual identity. *Journal of the American Psychoanalytic Association*, 6, 136–139.

Mahler, M. (1963). Some thoughts about development and individuation. *Psychoanalytic Study of the Child*, *18*, 307–324.

Mahler, M. (1967). On human symbiosis and the vicissitudes of individuation. *Journal of the American Psychoanalytic Association*, *15*, 740–763.

Mahler, M. (1968). *On human symbiosis and the vissisitudes of individuation: Vol. 1. Infantile psychosis*. New York: International Universities Press.

Mahler, M. (1972). The rapprochement subphase of the separation-individuation process. *Psychoanalytic Quarterly*, *41*, 487–506.

Mahler, M., Pine, F., & Bergman, A. (1975). *The psychological birth of the human infant*. New York: Basic Books.

Malmstrom, P. M. (1978). *Some influences of twinship in the language of toddlers*. Unpublished manuscript.

Manosevitz, M., Lindzey, C., & Thiessen, D. D. (Eds.). (1969). *Behavioral genetics*. New York: Appleton-Century-Crofts.

Marks, I. M., Crowe, M., Drewe, E., Young, J., & Dewhurst, W. G. (1969). Obsessive-complusive neurosis in identical twins. *British Journal of Psychology*, *115*, 991–998.

Martin, T. O., & Gross, R. B. (1979). A comparison of twins for degree of closeness and field dependence. *Adolescence*, *14*, 739–745.

Matas, L., Arend, R. A., & Sroufe, L. A. (1978). Continuity of adaptation in the second year: The relationship between quality of attachment and later competence. *Child Development*, *49*, 547–556.

Matheny, A. P., & Dolan, A. B. (1975). Persons, situations, and time: A genetic view of behavioral change in childhood. *Journal of Personality and Social Psychology*, *32*, 1106–1110.

Matheny, A. P., Dolan, A. B., & Wilson, R. S. (1976). Twins: Within-pair similarity on Bayley's Infant Behavior Record. *Journal of Genetic Psychology*, *128*, 263–270.

Matheny, A. P., Wilson, R. S., & Brown-Dolan, A. (1976). Relations between twins' similarity of appearance and behavioral similarity: Testing an assumption. *Behavioral Genetics*, *6*, 343–351.

Matheny, A. P., Wilson, R. S., Dolan, A. B., & Krantz, J. Z. (1981). Behavioral contrasts in twinships: Stability and patterns of differences in childhood. *Child Development*, *52*, 579–588.

184

Meissner, W. W. (1981). *Internalization in psychoanalysis* (Psychological Issues Monograph No. 50). New York: International Universities Press.

Mittler, P. L. (1970). Biological and social aspects of language development in twins. *Developmental Medical Child Neurology*, *12*, 741–757.

Mittler, P. L. (1971). *The study of twins*. London: Penguin.

Modell, A. H. (1968). *Object love and reality: An introduction to a psychoanalytic theory of object relations*. New York: International Universities Press.

Myers, W. A. (1976). Imaginary companions, fantasy twins, mirror dreams, and depersonalization. *Psychoanalytic Quarterly*, *45*, 503–524.

Nagera, H. (1981). *The developmental approach to childhood psychopathology*. New York: Jason Aronson.

Newman, H. H., Freeman, F. N., & Holzinger, K. L. (1937). *Twins: A study of heredity and environment*. Chicago: University of Chicago Press.

Nichols, R. C. (1966). The resemblance of twins in personality and interests. *National Merit Scholarship Corporation Research Reports*, *2*, 1–23.

Nichols, R. C., & Bilbro, W. C. (1966). The diagnosis of twin zygosity. *Acta Genetica*, *16*, 265–275.

Orr, D. (1941). A psychoanalytic study of a fraternal twin. *Psychoanalytic Quarterly*, *10*, 284–296.

Paluszny, M., & Abelson, A. G. (1975). Twins in a child psychiatric clinic. *American Journal of Psychiatry*, *132*, 434–436.

Paluszny, M., & Baeit-Hallahmi, B. (1974). An assessment of monozygotic twin relationships by the semantic differential. *Archives of General Psychiatry*, *31*, 110–112.

Paluszny, M., & Gibson, R. (1974). Twin interaction in a normal nursery school. *American Journal of Psychiatry*, *131*, 293–296.

Paluszny, M., Selzer, M., Vinokur, A., & Lewandowski, L. (1977). Twin relationships and depression. *American Journal of Psychiatry*, *134*, 988–990.

Pasamanick, B., & Knoblock, H. (1961). In G. Caplan (Ed.), *Prevention of mental disorders in children*. New York: Basic Books.

Peery, J. C. (1978). Effects of different situations on mother-infant gazing. *Child Study Journal*, 8, 111–121.

Piaget, J. (1937). *The construction of reality in the child*. New York: Basic Books.

Plomin, R. A. (1976). A twin and family study of personality in young children. *Journal of Psychology*, 94, 233–235.

Plomin, R., & Rowe, D. G. (1977). A twin study of temperament in young children. *Journal of Psychology*, 97, 107–113.

Plomin, R., & Rowe, D. G. (1978). Genes, environment, and the development of temperament in young human twins. In G. M. Burghardt & M. Bekoff (Eds.), *The development of behavior*. New York: Garland Press.

Plomin, R., & Rowe, D. G. (1979). Genetic and environmental etiology of social behavior in infancy. *Developmental Psychology*, 15, 62–72.

Plomin, R., Willerman, L., & Loehlin, J. C. (1976). Resemblance in appearance and the equal environments assumption in twin studies of personality traits. *Behavioral Genetics*, 6, 43–52.

Price, B. (1950). Primary biases in twin studies: A review of prenatal and natal difference-producing factors in monozygotic pairs. *American Journal of Genetics*, 2, 293–352.

Record, R. G., McKeown, T., & Edwards, J. H. (1970). An investigation of the difference in measured intelligence between twins and single births. *Annals of Human Genetics*, 34, 11–20.

Resnikoff, M., Domino, G., Bridges, C., & Honeyman, M. (1973). Perceptions of alikeness and attitudes toward being a twin: Comparison of identical and fraternal twin pairs. *Perceptual and Motor Skills*, 37, 103–106.

Richards, T. W., & Simons, M. P. (1941). The Fels child behavior scales. *Genetic Psychology Monographs*, 24, 259–309.

Roberts, C. A., & Johansson, C. B. (1974). The inheritance of cognitive interest styles among twins. *Journal of Vocational Behavior*, 4, 237–243.

Rutter, M. (1970). Psychological development: Predictions from infancy. *Journal of Child Psychology and Psychiatry*, 11, 49.

Rutter, M., Korn, S., & Birch, H. G. (1963). Genetic and environmental factors in the development of primary reaction patterns. *British Journal of Social and Clinical Psychology*, 2, 161–173.

186

Savic, S., & Jocic, M. (1975). Some features of dialogue between twins. *International Journal of Psycholinguistics*, 4, 33–51.

Scarr, S. (1966). Genetic factors in activity motivation. *Child Development*, 37, 663–673.

Scarr, S. (1969). Social introversion-extroversion as a heritable response. *Child Development*, 40, 823–83.

Scarr, S., & Carter-Saltzman, L. (1979). Twin method: defense of a critical assumption. *Behavioral Genetics*, 9, 527–542.

Schachter, F. F., Gilutz, G., Shore, E., & Adler, M. (1978). Sibling deidentification judged by mothers: Cross validation and developmental studies. *Child Development*, 49, 543–546.

Schachter, F. F., Shore, E., Feldman-Rotman, S., Marquis, R. E., & Campbell, S. (1976). Sibling deidentification. *Developmental Psychology*, 12, 418–427.

Scheinfeld, A. (1967). *Twins and supertwins*. Philadelphia: Lippincott.

Schwartz, M., & Schwartz, J. (1974). Evidence against a genetical component to performance on IQ tests. *Nature*, 248, 84–85.

Shields, J. (1954). Personality differences and neurotic traits in normal twin school children. *Eugenics Review*, 45, 213–245.

Shields, J. (1962). *Monozygotic twins. brought up apart and brought up together: An investigation into the genetic and environmental causes of variation in personality*. London: Oxford University Press.

Silverman, M. A. (1980). The first year after birth. In S. I. Greenspan & G. H. Pollock (Eds.). *The course of life: Psychoanalytic contributions toward understanding personality development: Vol. 1*. Bethesda: National Institute of Mental Health.

Slater, E., & Cowie, V. (1971). *The genetics of mental disorders*. London: Oxford University Press.

Smith, G. (1949). The psychological studies in twin differences. *Studia psychologa pedagogica* (Vol. 3). Antwerp: Standaard.

Smith, R. T. (1965). A comparison of socio-environmental factors in monozygotic and dizygotic twins, testing an assumption. In S. G. Vandenberg (Ed.), *Methods and goals in human behavior genetics*. New York: Academic Press.

Smock, D. C., & Holt, B. G. (1962). Children's reactions to novelty. *Child Development*, 33, 631–642.

Spitz, R. A. (1946). The smiling response: A contribution to the ontogenesis of social relations. *Genetic Psychology Monographs*, *34*, 57–125.

Spitz, R. A. (1965). *The first year of life: A psychoanalytic study of normal and deviant development of object relations.* New York: International Universities Press.

Sroufe, L. A., & Waters, E. (1977). Attachment as an organizational construct. *Child Development*, *48*, 1184–1199.

Stern, D. (1974). Mother and infant at play: The dyadic interaction involving facial, vocal and gaze behavior. In M. Lewis & L. Rosenblum (Eds.), *The effects of the infant on its caregiver.* New York: Wiley.

Sugar, M. (1982). *The premature in context.* Jamaica, NY: Spectrum.

Sweet, A. Y. (1973). Classification of the low-birth-weight infant. In M. Klaus & A. Fanaroff (Eds.), *The care of the high-risk neonate.* Philadelphia: W. B. Saunders.

Terry, G. (1975). The separation-individuation process in same-sex twins: A review of the literature. *Maternal-Child Nursing Journal*, *4*, 121–128.

Thomas, A., Birch, S. A., Chess, H. G., Hertzog, M., and Korn, S. (1964). *Behavioral individuality in early childhood.* London: University of London Press.

Thomas, A. & Chess, S. (1977). *Temperament and development.* New York: Brunner-Mazel.

Thurstone, T. G., Thurstone, L. L., & Strandkov, H. H. (1955). *A psychological study of twins.* Chapel Hill: University of North Carolina Press.

Tienari, P. (1963). Psychiatric illness in identical twins. *Acta Psychiatrica*, *171*.

Torgersen, A. M., & Kringlen, E. (1978). Genetic aspects of temperamental differences in infants: A study of same-sexed twins. *American Academy of Child Psychiatry*, *17*, 433–444.

Van Valen, L. (1979). Heritability of intelligence. *Journal of Biological Psychology*, *21*, 206–221.

Vandenberg, S. G. (1962). The hereditary abilities study: Hereditary components in a psychological test battery. *American Journal of Human Genetics*, *14*, 220–237.

Vandenberg, S. G. (Ed.). (1965). *Methods and goals in human behavior.* New York: Academic Press.

Vandenberg, S. G. (1966). The contribution of twin research to psychology. *Psychological Bulletin*, 66, 327–352.

Vandenberg, S. G. (1967). Hereditary factors in normal personality traits as measured by inventories. In J. Wortis (Ed.), *Recent advances in biological psychiatry*. New York: Plenum.

Vandenberg, S. G., & Johnson, R. C. (1968). Further evidence on the relation between age of separation and similarity in IQ among pairs of separated identical twins. In S. Vandenberg (Ed.), *Progress in human behavior genetics*. Baltimore: The Johns Hopkins University Press.

Vernon, P. E. (1960). *Intelligence attainment and tests*. London: University of London Press.

Wilson, R. (1974). Twins: Mental development in the preschool years. *Developmental Psychology*, 10, 580–588.

Wilson, R. (1975). Twins: Patterns of cognitive development as measures of Wechsler preschool and primary scale of intelligence. *Developmental Psychology*, 11, 126–134.

Wilson, R. (1977). Twins and siblings: Concordance for school-age mental development. *Child Development*, 48, 211–216.

Wilson, R. (1978). Synchronies in mental development: An epigenetic perspective. *Science*, 202, 939–948.

Wilson, R., Brown, A. M., & Matheny, A. (1971). Emergence and persistence of behavioral differences in twins. *Child Development*, 42, 1381–1398.

Wilson, R., & Matheny, A. P. (1983). Assessment of temperament in infant twins. *Developmental Psychology*, 19, 172–183.

Winnicott, D. W. (1953). Transitional objects and transitional phenomena: A study of the first not-me possession. *International Journal of Psycho-Analysis*, 34, 89–97.

Winnicott, D. W. (1960). *The family and individual development*. New York: Basic Books.

Winnicott, D. W. (1962). *The maturational processes and the facilitating environment*. New York: International Universities Press.

Winnicott, D. W. (1964). *The child, the family and the outside world*. London: Penguin Books.

Winnicott, D. W. (1977). *The Piggle*. London: Hogarth Press.

Yerushalmy, J., & Sheerar, S. E. (1940). Studies in twins: The reaction of order of birth and age of parent to the frequency of like-sexed and unlike-sexed twin deliveries. *Human Biology*, *12*, 95–113.

Zazzo, R. (1960). *Les jumeaux, le coutle, et la personne.* Paris: Presses Universitaires de France.

Zuger, M. (1976). Monozygotic twins discordant for homosexuality: Report of a pair and significance of the phenomenon. *Comprehensive Psychiatry*, *17*, 661–669.

Appendix A: Description of Sample

Monozygotic Twins

Name	Age
1. Cindy and Lindy	18
2. Vickie and Valery	19
3. Charles and Frank *	21
4. Tim and Tom	25
5. Jean and Sandie	25
6. Melissa and Stephanie	26
7. Darla and Marla *	31
8. Fred and Ted	33
9. Henri and Ian	45
10. Ralph and Mark **	72

Total Actually Interviewed = 17 (8 Male, 9 Female)

* Geographic distance precluded participation in the study.
** Deceased.

Dizygotic Twins, Same Sex

Name	Age
1. Bob and Dave	14
2. Dianne and Debbie	22
3. Margerie and Melanie	30

Total Actually Interviewed = 6 (2 Male, 4 Female)

Dizygotic Twins, Opposite Sex

Name	Age
1. Martha and John *	28
2. Amy and Steve	29

Total Actually Interviewed = 3 (1 Male, 2 Female)

* Geographic distance precluded participation in the study.

Average Age of Sample = 27.8 Years

Total Number of Twins Interviewed = 26

Number of Twinships Represented = 15

Appendix B: Questionnaire

1. Name

2. Age

3. Education: (check one) elementary school
                           high school
                           college
                           professional school

4. How many siblings do you have?

5. Is there any history of twins in your family? If so, who?

6. (If married) Husband's name

7. Age

8. Education: (check one) elementary school
                           high school
                           college
                           professional school

9. How many siblings does your husband have?

10. Is there any history of twins in his family? If so, who?

11. Before you had twins, what were your attitudes about twins in general? (Please try to be as specific as you can.)

12. When did you first find out you were having twins? (What month during your pregnancy?)

13. When you found out you were having twins, how did you feel?

14. When your husband found out you were having twins, how did he feel?

15. Age of twins: _____ years _____ months

16. Sex(es)

17. They are: (circle one)
    identical   same-sex fraternal   opposite-sex fraternal

18. List your other children who are older than the twins (include sex and age).

19. List your other children who are younger than the twins (include sex and age).

20. What did your doctor tell you concerning your twins being identical or fraternal?

21. What are the twins' names?
    Birth weight: _____ lbs. _____ ozs.

22. Why were each of these names chosen?

23. Who was born first?

24. What was the time difference between the births?

25. Were there any complications during pregnancy or delivery?

26. Was either twin considered premature?

27. If so, did either have to spend extra time in the hospital? Who, and how long?

28. Do either of the twins have any physical or medical problems?

29. Describe how feeding the twins was accomplished during infancy (e.g., breast- or bottle-fed, did one twin usually go first, how did you keep track of who was fed, etc?)

30. Rate the following people according to how involved they were in child care during the twins' infancy.

	not involved at all				extremely involved
	0	1	2	3	4
father					
grandmother					
older sibling					
other _____					

31. When did each of the twins begin to: (be specific with respect to ages)

	Who first?	When?	Who second?	When?
Crawl				
Walk				
Talk (single words)				
use two or more words)				

32. Describe what was most rewarding for you as a mother when the twins were infants.

33. Describe what was most difficult for you as a mother when the twins were infants.

Twins learn to interact and recognize each other in stages. At approximately what age did your twins:

34. (a) seem to derive a special pleasure in being with each other as infants? (Give examples.)

35. (b) actually make up games that they played together? (Give examples.)

36. Do the twins know they are twins? If so, what indications do you have? At what age did they first become aware of this? (Give examples.)

37. Rivalry plays a role in most sibling relationships. How often do you feel it plays a role in the twin relationship? (Place a check at the appropriate point.)

1	2	3	4	5
never	sometimes	moderately often	often	always

38. Give as many examples as you can.

39. Do the twins ever get confused about who is whom? Give as many examples as you can.

40. How do the twins feel about being separated from each other? Give examples.

41. How do the twins feel about being separated from you? Give examples.

42. Did either of the twins choose a favorite object, such as a blanket or toy, to use for comfort or to fall asleep with? Describe.

43. Did either of the twins have an imaginary companion? Describe.

44. Did the twins have a private language? Describe.

45. If they did have a private language, did anyone serve as translator for other family members?

46. Do the twins look alike? How difficult is it to tell them apart?

47. Have you or your husband ever mixed them up? What happened?

48. Do you dress the twins alike? How frequently? What is your reason for this?

How do other people react to the twins?

49. Siblings

50. Extended family

51. Friends

52. Strangers

53. In terms of their personalities, how are the twins similar?

54. In terms of their personalities, how are the twins different?

55. Does one twin typically depend on the other? Describe.

56. How do you treat the twins differently from the way you treat your other children?

57. How does each twin resemble you or your husband?

58. Is there anyone else that they take after?

59. What kind of relationship do you expect the twins to have with each other when they're grown?

60. Will the twins be (have the twins been) placed in the same or different classrooms in school? What is your opinion about this?

61. Are you concerned about the twins' developing separate identities? What are your thoughts about this?

62. Are there issues in the twins' growing up that concern you? Describe.

63. What advice do you have for other mothers of twins?

64. Any additional comments?

Index